J. V. STALIN

ANARCHISM or SOCIALISM?

From J. V. Stalin, *Works*,
Foreign Languages Publishing House,
Moscow, 1954,
Vol. 1, pp. 297-391.

Reprinted by Red Star Publishers
United States of America, 2017
www.RedStarPublishers.org

CONTENTS

ANARCHISM OR SOCIALISM?

ANARCHISM OR SOCIALISM? [1]

The hub of modern social life is the class struggle. In the course of this struggle each class is guided by its own ideology. The bourgeoisie has its own ideology – so-called *liberalism*. The proletariat also has its own ideology – this, as is well known, is *socialism*.

Liberalism must not be regarded as something whole and indivisible: it is subdivided into different trends, corresponding to the different strata of the bourgeoisie.

Nor is socialism whole and indivisible: in it there are also different trends.

We shall not here examine liberalism – that task had better be left for another time. We want to acquaint the reader only with socialism and its trends. We think that he will find this more interesting.

Socialism is divided into three main trends: *reformism*, *anarchism* and *Marxism*.

Reformism (Bernstein and others), which regards socialism as a remote goal and nothing more, reformism, which actually repudiates the socialist revolution and aims at establishing socialism by peaceful means, reformism, which advocates not class struggle but class collaboration – this reformism is decaying day by day, is day by day losing all semblance of socialism and, in our opinion, it is totally unnecessary to examine it in these articles when defining socialism.

It is altogether different with Marxism and anarchism: both are at the present time recognised as socialist trends, they are waging a fierce struggle against each other, both are trying to present themselves to the proletariat as genuinely socialist doctrines, and, of course, a study and comparison of the two will be far more interesting for the reader.

We are not the kind of people who, when the word "anarchism" is mentioned, turn away contemptuously and say with a supercilious wave of the hand: "Why waste time on that, it's not worth talking about!" We think that such cheap "criticism" is undignified and useless.

Nor are we the kind of people who console themselves with the thought that the Anarchists "have no masses behind them and, therefore, are not so dangerous." It is not who has a larger or smaller "mass" following today, but the essence of the doctrine that matters. If the "doctrine" of the Anarchists expresses the truth, then it goes without saying that it will certainly hew a path for itself and will rally the masses around itself. If, however, it is unsound and built up on a false foundation, it will not last long and will remain suspended in mid-air. But the unsoundness of anarchism must be proved.

Some people believe that Marxism and anarchism are based on the same principles and that the disagreements between them concern only tactics, so that, in the opinion of these people, it is quite impossible to draw a contrast between these two trends.

This is a great mistake.

We believe that the Anarchists are real enemies of Marxism. Accordingly, we also hold that a real struggle must be waged against real enemies. Therefore, it is necessary to examine the "doctrine" of the Anarchists from beginning to end and weigh it up thoroughly from all aspects.

The point is that Marxism and anarchism are built up on entirely different principles, in spite of the fact that both come into the arena of the struggle under the flag of socialism. The cornerstone of anarchism is the *individual*, whose emancipation, according to its tenets, is the principal condition for the emancipation of the masses, the collective body. According to the tenets of anarchism, the emancipation of the masses is impossible until the individual is emancipated. Accordingly, its slogan is: "Everything for the individual." The cornerstone of Marxism, however, is the *masses*, whose emancipation, according to its tenets, is the principal condition for the emancipation of the individual. That is to say, according to the tenets of Marxism, the emancipation of the individual is impossible until the masses are emancipated. Accordingly, its slogan is: "Everything for the masses."

Clearly, we have here two principles, one negating the other, and not merely disagreements on tactics.

The object of our articles is to place these two opposite principles side by side, to compare Marxism with anarchism, and thereby throw light on their respective virtues and defects. At this point we think it necessary to acquaint the reader with the plan of these articles.

We shall begin with a description of Marxism, deal, in passing, with the Anarchists' views on Marxism, and then proceed to criticise anarchism itself. Namely: we shall expound the dialectical method, the Anarchists' views on this method, and our criticism; the materialist theory, the Anarchists' views and our criticism (here, too, we shall discuss the socialist revolution, the socialist dictatorship, the minimum programme, and tactics generally); the philosophy of the Anarchists and our criticism; the socialism of the Anarchists and our criticism; anarchist tactics and organisation – and, in conclusion, we shall give our deductions.

We shall try to prove that, as advocates of small community socialism, the Anarchists are not genuine Socialists.

We shall also try to prove that, in so far as they repudiate the dictatorship of the proletariat, the Anarchists are also not genuine revolutionaries....

And so, let us proceed with our subject.

I

THE DIALECTICAL METHOD

Everything in the world is in motion....
Life changes, productive forces grow,
old relations collapse.

Karl Marx

Marxism is not only the theory of socialism, it is an integral world outlook, a philosophical system, from which Marx's proletarian socialism logically follows. This philosophical system is called dialectical materialism.

Hence, to expound Marxism means to expound also dialectical materialism.

Why is this system called dialectical materialism?

Because its *method* is dialectical, and its *theory* is materialistic.

What is the dialectical method?

It is said that social life is in continual motion and development. And that is true: life must not be regarded as something immutable and static; it never remains at one level, it is in eternal motion, in an eternal process of destruction and creation. Therefore, life always contains the *new* and the *old*, the *growing* and the *dying*, the revolutionary and the counter-revolutionary.

The dialectical method tells us that we must regard life as it actually is. We have seen that life is in continual motion; consequently, we must regard life in its motion and ask: Where is life going? We have seen that life presents a picture of constant destruction and creation; consequently, we must examine life in its process of destruction and creation and ask: What is being destroyed and what is being created in life?

That which in life is born and grows day by day is invincible, its progress cannot be checked. That is to say, if, for example, in life the proletariat as a class is born and grows day by day, no matter how weak and small in numbers it may be *today*, in the long run it must triumph. Why? Because it is growing, gaining strength and marching forward. On the other hand, that which in life is growing old and advancing to its grave must inevitably suffer defeat, even if *today* it represents a titanic force. That is to say, if, for example, the bourgeoisie is gradually losing ground and is slipping farther and farther back every day, then, no matter how strong and numerous it may be today, it must, in the long run, suffer defeat. Why? Because as a class it is decaying, growing feeble, growing old, and becoming a burden to life.

Hence arose the well-known dialectical proposition: all that which really exists, i.e., all that which grows day by day is rational, and all that which decays day by day is irrational and, consequently, cannot avoid defeat.

For example. In the eighties of the last century a great controversy flared up among the Russian revolutionary intelligentsia. The Narodniks asserted that the main force that could undertake the task of "emancipating Russia" was the petty bourgeoisie, rural and urban. Why? – the Marxists asked them. Because, answered the Narodniks, the rural and urban petty bourgeoisie now constitute the majority and, moreover, they are poor, they live in poverty.

To this the Marxists replied: It is true that the rural and urban petty bourgeoisie now constitute the majority and are really poor, but is that the point? The petty bourgeoisie has long constituted the majority, but up to now it has displayed no initiative in the struggle for "freedom" without the assistance of the proletariat. Why? Because the petty bourgeoisie as a class is not growing; on the contrary, it is disintegrating day by day and breaking up into bourgeois and proletarians. On the other hand, nor is poverty of decisive importance here, of course: "tramps" are poorer than the petty bourgeoisie, but nobody will say that they can undertake the task of "emancipating Russia."

As you see, the point is not which class today constitutes the majority, or which class is poorer, but which class is gaining strength and which is decaying.

And as the proletariat is the only class which is steadily growing and gaining strength, which is pushing social life forward and rallying all the revolutionary elements around itself, our duty is to regard it as the main force in the present-day movement, join its ranks and make its progressive strivings our strivings.

That is how the Marxists answered.

Obviously the Marxists looked at life dialectically, whereas the Narodniks argued metaphysically – they pictured social life as having become static at a particular stage.

That is how the dialectical method looks upon the development of life.

But there is movement and movement. There was movement in social life during the "December days," when the proletariat, straightening its back, stormed arms depots and launched an attack upon reaction. But the movement of preceding years, when the proletariat, under the conditions of "peaceful" development, limited itself to individual strikes and the formation of small trade unions, must also be called social movement.

Clearly, movement assumes different forms.

And so the dialectical method says that movement has two forms: the evolutionary and the revolutionary form.

Movement is evolutionary when the progressive elements spontaneously continue their daily activities and introduce minor, *quantitative* changes into the old order.

Movement is revolutionary when the same elements combine, become imbued with a single idea and sweep down upon the enemy camp with the object of uprooting the old order and of introducing *qualitative* changes in life, of establishing a new order.

Evolution prepares for revolution and creates the ground for it; revolution consummates the process of evolution and facilitates its further activity.

Similar processes take place in nature. The history of science shows that the dialectical method is a truly scientific method: from astronomy to sociology, in every field we find confirmation of the idea that nothing is eternal in the universe, everything changes, everything develops. Consequently, everything in nature must be regarded from the point of view of movement, development. And this means that the spirit of dialectics permeates the whole of present-day science.

As regards the forms of movement, as regards the fact that according to dialectics, minor, quantitative changes sooner or later lead to major, qualitative changes – this law applies with equal force to the history of nature. Mendeleyev's "periodic system of elements" clearly shows how very important in the history of nature is the emergence of *qualitative* changes out of *quantitative* changes. The same thing is shown in biology by the theory of neo-Lamarckism, to which neo-Darwinism is yielding place.

We shall say nothing about other facts, on which F. Engels has thrown sufficiently full light in his *Anti-Dühring*.

Such is the content of the dialectical method.

* * *

How do the Anarchists look upon the dialectical method?

Everybody knows that Hegel was the father of the dialectical method. Marx purged and improved this method. The Anarchists are aware of this, of course. They know that Hegel was a conservative, and so, taking advantage of this, they vehemently revile Hegel as a supporter of "restoration, " they try with the utmost zeal to "prove" that "Hegel is a philosopher of restoration... that he eulogizes bureaucratic constitutionalism in its absolute form, that the general idea of his philosophy of history is subordinate to and serves the philosophical trend of the period of restoration," and so on and so forth (see *Nobati*,[2] No. 6. Article by V. Cherkezishvili.)

The well-known Anarchist Kropotkin tries to "prove" the same thing in his works (see, for example, his *Science and Anarchism*, in Russian).

Our Kropotkinites, from Cherkezishvili right down to Sh. G., all with one voice echo Kropotkin (see *Nobati*).

True, nobody contests what they say on this point; on the contrary, everybody agrees that Hegel was not a revolutionary. Marx and Engels themselves proved before anybody else did, in their *Critique of Critical Criticism*, that Hegel's views on history fundamentally contradict the idea of the sovereignty of the people. But in spite of this, the Anarchists go on trying to "prove," and deem it necessary to go on day in and day out trying to "prove," that Hegel was a supporter of "restoration." Why do they do this? Probably, in order by all this to discredit Hegel and make their readers feel that the "reactionary" Hegel's method also cannot be other than "repugnant" and unscientific.

The Anarchists think that they can refute the dialectical method in this way.

We affirm that in this way they can prove nothing but their own ignorance. Pascal and Leibnitz were not revolutionaries, but the mathematical method they discovered is recognised today as a scientific method. Mayer and Helmholtz were not revolutionaries, but their discoveries in the field of physics became the basis of science. Nor were Lamarck and Darwin revolutionaries, but their evolutionary method put biological science on its feet.... Why, then, should the fact not be admitted that, in spite of his conservatism, Hegel succeeded in working out a scientific method which is called the dialectical method?

No, *in this way* the Anarchists will prove nothing but their own ignorance.

To proceed. In the opinion of the Anarchists, "dialectics is metaphysics," and as they "want to free science from metaphysics, philosophy from theology," they repudiate the dialectical method (see *Nobati*, Nos. 3 and 9. Sh. G. See also Kropotkin's *Science and Anarchism*).

Oh, those Anarchists! As the saying goes: "Blame others for your own sins." Dialectics matured in the struggle against metaphysics and gained fame in this struggle; but according to the Anarchists, dialectics is metaphysics!

Dialectics tells us that nothing in the world is eternal, everything in the world is transient and mutable; nature changes, society changes, habits and customs change, conceptions of justice change, truth itself changes – that is why dialectics regards everything critically; that is why it denies the existence of a once-and-for-all established truth. Consequently, it also repudiates abstract "dogmatic propositions, which, once discovered, had merely to be learned by heart" (see F. Engels, *Ludwig Feuerbach*). [3]

Metaphysics, however, tells us something altogether different. From its standpoint the world is something eternal and immutable (see F. Engels, *Anti-Dühring*), it has been once and for all determined by someone or something – that is why the metaphysicians always have "eternal justice" or "immutable truth" on their lips.

Proudhon, the "father" of the Anarchists, said that there existed in the world an *immutable justice determined once and for all*, which must be made the basis of future society. That is why Proudhon has been called a metaphysician. Marx fought Proudhon with the aid of the dialectical method and proved that since everything in the world changes, "justice" must also change, and that, consequently, "immutable justice" is metaphysical nonsense (see K. Marx, *The Poverty of Philosophy*). The Georgian disciples of the metaphysician Proudhon, however, keep reiterating that "Marx's dialectics is metaphysics"!

Metaphysics recognises various nebulous dogmas, such as, for example, the "unknowable," the "thing-in itself," and, in the long run, passes into empty theology. In contrast to Proudhon and Spencer, Engels combated these dogmas with the aid of the dialectical method (see *Ludwig Feuerbach*); but the Anarchists – the disciples of Proudhon and Spencer – tell us that Proudhon and Spencer were scientists, whereas Marx and Engels were metaphysicians!

One of two things: either the Anarchists are deceiving themselves, or else they do not know what they are talking about.

At all events, it is beyond doubt that the Anarchists confuse Hegel's *metaphysical* system with his *dialectical* method.

Needless to say, Hegel's *philosophical system*, which rests on the immutable idea, is from beginning to end *metaphysical*. But it is also clear that Hegel's *dialectical method*, which repudiates all immutable ideas, is from beginning to end *scientific* and *revolutionary*.

That is why Karl Marx, who subjected Hegel's metaphysical system to devastating criticism, at the same time praised his dialectical method, which, as Marx said, "lets nothing impose upon it, and is in its essence critical and revolutionary" (see *Capital*, Vol. I. Preface).

That is why Engels sees a big difference between Hegel's method and his system. "Whoever placed the chief emphasis on the Hegelian *system* could be fairly conservative in both spheres; whoever regarded the dialectical *method* as the main thing could belong to the most extreme opposition, both in politics and religion" (see *Ludwig Feuerbach*).

The Anarchists fail to see this difference and thoughtlessly maintain that "dialectics is metaphysics."

16

To proceed. The Anarchists say that the dialectical method is "subtle word-weaving," "the method of sophistry," "logical somersaults" (see *Nobati*, No. 8. Sh. G.), "with the aid of which both truth and falsehood are proved with equal facility" (see *Nobati*, No. 4. Article by V. Cherkezishvili).

Thus, in the opinion of the Anarchists, the dialectical method proves both truth and falsehood.

At first sight it would seem that the accusation advanced by the Anarchists has some foundation. Listen, for example, to what Engels says about the follower of the metaphysical method:

"...His communication is: 'Yea, yea; nay, nay, for whatsoever is more than these cometh of evil.' For him a thing either exists, or it does not exist; it is equally impossible for a thing to be itself and at the same time something else. Positive and negative absolutely exclude one another..." (see *Anti-Dühring*, Introduction).

How is that? – the Anarchists cry heatedly. Is it possible for a thing to be good and bad at the same time?! That is "sophistry," "juggling with words," it shows that "you want to prove truth and falsehood with equal facility"!...

Let us, however, go into the substance of the matter.

Today we are demanding a democratic republic. Can we say that a democratic republic is good in all respects, or bad in all respects? No we cannot! Why? Because a democratic republic is good only in one respect: when it destroys the feudal system; but it is bad in another respect: when it strengthens the bourgeois system. Hence we say: in so far as the democratic republic destroys the feudal system it is good – and we fight for it; but in so far as it strengthens the bourgeois system it is bad – and we fight against it.

So the same democratic republic can be "good" and "bad" at the same time – it is "yes" and "no."

The same thing may be said about the eight-hour day, which is good and bad at the same time: "good" in so far as it strengthens the proletariat, and "bad" in so far as it strengthens the wage system.

It was facts of this kind that Engels had in mind when he characterised the dialectical method in the words we quoted above.

The Anarchists, however, fail to understand this, and an absolutely clear idea seems to them to be nebulous "sophistry."

The Anarchists are, of course, at liberty to note or ignore these *facts*, they may even ignore the sand on the sandy seashore – they have every right to do that. But why drag in the dialectical method, which, unlike anarchism, does not look at life with its eyes shut, which has its finger on the pulse of life and openly says: since life changes and is in motion, every phenomenon of life has two trends: a positive and a negative; the first we must defend, the second we must reject.

To proceed further. In the opinion of our Anarchists, "dialectical development is catastrophic development, by means of which, first the past is utterly destroyed, and then the future is established quite separately.... Cuvier's cataclysms were due to unknown causes, but Marx and Engels's catastrophes are engendered by dialectics" (see *Nobati*, No. 8. Sh. G.).

In another place the same author writes: "Marxism rests on Darwinism and treats it uncritically" (see *Nobati*, No. 6). Now listen!

Cuvier rejects Darwin's theory of evolution, he recognises only cataclysms, and cataclysms are *unexpected* upheavals "due to *unknown* causes." The Anarchists say that the Marxists *adhere to Cuvier's view* and therefore *repudiate Darwinism*.

Darwin rejects Cuvier's cataclysms, he recognises gradual evolution. But the same Anarchists say that "Marxism rests on Darwinism and treats it uncritically," i.e., the Marxists repudiate *Cuvier's cataclysms*.

In short, the Anarchists accuse the Marxists of adhering to Cuvier's view and at the same time reproach them for adhering to Darwin's and not to Cuvier's view.

This is anarchy if you like! As the saying goes: the Sergeant's widow flogged herself! Clearly, Sh. G. of No. 8 of *Nobati* forgot what Sh. G. of No. 6 said.

Which is right: No. 8 or No. 6?

Let us turn to the facts. Marx says:

"At a certain stage of their development, the material productive forces of society come in conflict with the existing relations of production, or – what is but a legal expression for the same thing – with the property relations.... Then begins an epoch of social revolution." But "no social order ever perishes before all the productive forces for which there is room in it have developed..." (see K. Marx, *A Contribution to the Critique of Political Economy*. Preface).[4]

If this thesis of Marx is applied to modern social life, we shall find that between the present-day productive forces, which are *social* in character, and the form of appropriation of the product, which is *private* in character, there is a fundamental conflict which must culminate in the socialist revolution (see F. Engels, *Anti-Dühring*, Part III, Chapter II).

As you see, in the opinion of Marx and Engels, revolution is engendered not by Cuvier's "unknown causes," but by very definite and vital social causes called "the development of the productive forces."

As you see, in the opinion of Marx and Engels, revolution comes only when the productive forces have sufficiently matured, and not *unexpectedly*, as Cuvier thought.

Clearly, there is nothing in common between Cuvier's cataclysms and Marx's dialectical method.

On the other hand, Darwinism repudiates not only Cuvier's cataclysms, but also dialectically understood development, which includes revolution; whereas, from the standpoint of the dialectical method, evolution and revolution, quantitative and qualitative changes, are two essential forms of the same motion.

Obviously, it is also wrong to assert that "Marxism... treats Darwinism uncritically."

It turns out therefore, that *Nobati* is wrong in both cases, in No. 6 as well as in No. 8.

Lastly, the Anarchists tell us reproachfully that "dialectics... provides no possibility of getting, or jumping, out of oneself, or of jumping over oneself" (see *Nobati*, No. 8. Sh. G.).

Now that is the downright truth, Messieurs Anarchists! Here you are absolutely right, my dear sirs: the dialectical method does not, indeed, provide such a possibility. But why not? Because "jumping out of oneself, or jumping over oneself" is an exercise for wild goats, while the dialectical method was created for human beings.

That is the secret!...

Such, in general, are the Anarchists' views on the dialectical method.

Clearly, the Anarchists fail to understand the dialectical method of Marx and Engels; they have conjured up their own dialectics, and it is against this dialectics that they are fighting so ruthlessly.

All we can do is to laugh as we gaze at this spectacle, for one cannot help laughing when one sees a man fighting his own imagination, smashing his own inventions, while at the same time heatedly asserting that he is smashing his opponent.

II

THE MATERIALIST THEORY

*"It is not the consciousness of men that
determines their being, but, on the contrary,
their social being that determines their
consciousness."*

Karl Marx

We already know what the dialectical method is.

What is the materialist theory?

Everything in the world changes, everything in life develops, but *how* do these changes take place and *in what form* does this development proceed?

We know, for example, that the earth was once an incandescent, fiery mass; then it gradually cooled, plants and animals appeared, the development of the animal kingdom was followed by the appearance of a certain species of ape, and all this was followed by the appearance of man.

This, broadly speaking, is the way nature developed.

We also know that social life did not remain static either. There was a time when men lived on a primitive-communist basis; at that time they gained their livelihood by primitive hunting; they roamed through the forests and procured their food in that way. There came a time when primitive communism was superseded by the matriarchate – at that time men satisfied their needs mainly by means of primitive agriculture. Later the matriarchate was superseded by the patriarchate, under which men gained their livelihood mainly by cattle breeding. The patriarchate was later superseded by the slave-owning system – at that time men gained their livelihood by means of relatively more developed agriculture. The slave-owning system was followed by feudalism, and then, after all this, came the bourgeois system.

That, broadly speaking, is the way social life developed.

Yes, all this is well known.... But *how* did this development take place; did consciousness call forth the development of "nature" and of "society," or, on the contrary, did the development of "nature" and "society" call forth the development of consciousness?

This is how the materialist theory presents the question.

Some people say that "nature" and "social life" were preceded by the universal idea, which subsequently served as the basis of their development, so that the development of the phenomena of "nature" and of "social life" is, so to speak, the external form, merely the expression of the development of the universal idea.

Such, for example, was the doctrine of the *idealists*, who in the course of time split up into several trends.

Others say that from the very beginning there have existed in the world two mutually negating forces – idea and matter, consciousness and being, and that correspondingly, phenomena also fall into two categories – the ideal and the material, which negate each other, and contend against each other, so that the development of nature and society is a constant struggle between ideal and material phenomena.

Such, for example, was the doctrine of the *dualists*, who in the course of time, like the idealists, split up into several trends.

The materialist theory utterly repudiates both dualism and idealism.

Of course, both ideal and material phenomena exist in the world, but this does not mean that they negate each other. On the contrary, the ideal and the material sides are two different forms of one and the same nature or society, the one cannot be conceived without the other, they exist together, develop together, and, consequently, we have no grounds whatever for thinking that they negate each other.

Thus, so-called dualism proves to be unsound.

A single and indivisible nature expressed in two different forms – material and ideal; a single and indivisible social life expressed in two different forms – material and ideal – that is how we should regard the development of nature and of social life.

Such is the monism of the materialist theory.

At the same time, the materialist theory also repudiates idealism.

It is wrong to think that in its development the ideal side, and consciousness in general, precedes the development of the material side. So-called external "non-living" nature existed before there were any living beings. The first living matter possessed no consciousness, it possessed only *irritability* and the first rudiments of *sensation*. Later, animals gradually developed the power of sensation, which slowly passed into *consciousness*, in conformity with the development of the structure of their organisms and nervous systems. If the ape had always walked on all fours, if it had never stood upright, its descendant – man – would not have been able freely to use his lungs and vocal chords and, therefore, would not have been able to speak; and that would have fundamentally retarded the development of his consciousness. If, furthermore, the ape had not risen up on its hind legs, its descendant – man – would have been compelled always to walk on all fours, to look downwards and obtain his impressions only from there; he would have been unable to look up and around himself and, consequently, his brain would have obtained no more impressions than the brain of a quadruped. All this would have fundamentally retarded the development of human consciousness.

It follows, therefore, that the development of consciousness needs a particular structure of the organism and development of its nervous system.

It follows, therefore, that the development of the ideal side, the development of consciousness, is preceded by the development of the material side, the development of the external conditions: first the external conditions change, first the material side changes, and then consciousness, the ideal side, changes accordingly.

Thus, the history of the development of nature utterly refutes so-called idealism.

The same thing must be said about the history of the development of human society.

History shows that if at different times men were imbued with different ideas and desires, the reason for this is that at different times men fought nature in different ways to satisfy their needs and, accordingly, their economic relations assumed different forms. There was a time when men fought nature collectively, on the basis of primitive communism; at that time their property was communist property and, therefore, at that time they drew scarcely any distinction between "mine" and "thine," their consciousness was communistic. There came a time when the distinction between "mine" and "thine" penetrated the process of production; at that time property, too, assumed a private, individualist character and, therefore, the consciousness of men became imbued with the sense of private property. Then came the time, the present time, when production is again assuming a social character and, consequently, property, too, will soon assume a social character – and this is precisely why the consciousness of men is gradually becoming imbued with socialism.

Here is a simple illustration. Let us take a shoemaker who owned a tiny workshop, but who, unable to with stand the competition of the big manufacturers, closed his workshop and took a job, say, at Adelkhanov's shoe factory in Tiflis. He went to work at Adelkhanov's factory not with the view to becoming a permanent wage-worker, but with the object of saving up some money, of accumulating a little capital to enable him to reopen his workshop. As you see, the position of this shoemaker is *already* proletarian, but his consciousness is *still* non-proletarian, it is thoroughly petty-bourgeois. In other words, this shoemaker has *already* lost his petty-bourgeois position, it has gone, but his petty-bourgeois consciousness has *not yet* gone, it has lagged behind his actual position.

Clearly, here too, in social life, first the external conditions change, first the conditions of men change and then their consciousness changes accordingly.

But let us return to our shoemaker. As we already know, he intends to save up some money and then reopen his workshop. This proletarianised shoemaker goes on working, but finds that it is a very difficult matter to save money, because what he earns barely suffices to maintain an existence. Moreover, he realises that the opening of a private workshop is after all not so alluring: the rent he will have to pay for the premises, the caprices of customers, shortage of money, the competition of the big manufacturers and similar worries – such are the many troubles that torment the private workshop owner. On the other hand, the proletarian is relatively freer from such cares; he is not troubled by customers, or by having to pay rent for premises. He goes to the factory every morning, "calmly" goes home in the evening, and as calmly pockets his "pay" on Saturdays. Here, for the first time, the wings of our shoemaker's petty-bourgeois dreams are clipped; here for the first time proletarian strivings awaken in his soul.

Time passes and our shoemaker sees that he has not enough money to satisfy his most essential needs, that what he needs very badly is a rise in wages. At the same time, he hears his fellow-workers talking about unions and strikes. Here our shoemaker realises that in order to improve his conditions he must fight the masters and not open a workshop of his own. He joins the union, enters the strike movement, and soon becomes imbued with socialist ideas....

Thus, *in the long run*, the change in the shoemaker's material conditions was followed by a change in his consciousness: first his material conditions changed, and then, after a time, his consciousness changed accordingly.

The same must be said about classes and about society as a whole.

In social life, too, first the external conditions change, first the material conditions change, and then the ideas of men, their habits, customs and their world outlook change accordingly.

That is why Marx says:

"It is not the consciousness of men that determines their being, but, on the contrary, their social being that determines their consciousness."

If we can call the material side, the external conditions, being, and other phenomena of the same kind, the content, then we can call the ideal side, consciousness and other phenomena of the same kind, the form. Hence arose the well-known materialist proposition: in the process of development content precedes form, form lags behind content.

And as, in Marx's opinion, economic development is the "material foundation" of social life, its content, while legal-political and religious-philosophical development is the "ideological form" of this content, its "superstructure," Marx draws the conclusion that: "With the change of the economic foundation the entire immense superstructure is more or less rapidly transformed."

This, of course, does not mean that in Marx's opinion content is possible without form, as Sh. G. imagines (see *Nobati*, No. 1. "A Critique of Monism"). Content is impossible without form, but the point is that since a given form lags behind its content, it never *fully* corresponds to this content; and so the new content is "obliged" to clothe itself for a time in the old form, and this causes a conflict between them. At the present time, for example, the form of appropriation of the product, which is *private* in character, does not correspond to the *social* content of production, and this is the basis of the present-day social "conflict."

On the other hand, the idea that consciousness is a form of being does not mean that by its nature consciousness, too, is matter. That was the opinion held only by the vulgar materialists (for example, Büchner and Moleschott), whose theories fundamentally contradict Marx's materialism, and whom Engels rightly ridiculed in his *Ludwig Feuerbach*. According to Marx's materialism, consciousness and being, idea and matter, are two different forms of the same phenomenon, which, broadly speaking, is called nature, or society. Consequently, they do not negate each other;[*] nor are they one and the same phenomenon. The only point is that, in the development of nature and society, consciousness, i.e., what takes place in our heads, is preceded by a corresponding material change, i.e., what takes place outside of us; any given material change is, sooner or later, inevitably followed by a corresponding ideal change.

Very well, we shall be told, perhaps this is true as applied to the history of nature and society. But how do different conceptions and ideas arise in our heads at the present time? Do so-called external conditions really exist, or is it only our conceptions of these external conditions that exist? And if

---

[*] This does not contradict the idea that there is a conflict between form and content. The point is that the conflict is not between content and form in general, but between the *old* form and the *new* content, which is seeking a new form and is striving towards it.

external conditions exist, to what degree are they perceptible and cognizable?

On this point the materialist theory says that our conceptions, our "self," exist only in so far as external conditions exist that give rise to impressions in our "self." Whoever unthinkingly says that nothing exists but our conceptions, is compelled to deny the existence of all external conditions and, consequently, must deny the existence of all other people and admit the existence only of his own "self," which is absurd, and utterly contradicts the principles of science.

Obviously, external conditions do actually exist; these conditions existed before us, and will exist after us; and the more often and the more strongly they affect our consciousness, the more easily perceptible and cognizable do they become.

As regards the question as to how different conceptions and ideas arise in our heads at the present time, we must observe that here we have a repetition in brief of what takes place in the history of nature and society. In this case, too, the object outside of us preceded our conception of it; in this case, too, our conception, the form, lags behind the object – behind its content. When I look at a tree and see it – that only shows that this tree existed even before the conception of a tree arose in my head, that it was this tree that aroused the corresponding conception in my head....

Such, in brief, is the content of Marx's materialist theory.

The importance of the materialist theory for the practical activities of mankind can be readily understood.

If the economic conditions change *first* and the consciousness of men undergoes a corresponding change *later*, it is clear that we must seek the grounds for a given ideal not in the minds of men, not in their imaginations, but in the development of their economic conditions. Only that ideal is good and acceptable which is based on a study of economic conditions. All those ideals which ignore economic conditions and are not based upon their development are useless and unacceptable.

Such is the first practical conclusion to be drawn from the materialist theory.

If the consciousness of men, their habits and customs, are determined by external conditions, if the unsuitability of legal and political forms rests on an economic content, it is clear that we must help to bring about a radical change in economic relations in order, with this change, to bring about a radical change in the habits and customs of the people, and in their political system.

Here is what Karl Marx says on that score:

"No great acumen is required to perceive the necessary interconnection of materialism with... socialism. If man constructs all his knowledge, perceptions, etc., from the world of sense... then it follows that it is a question of so arranging the empirical world that he experiences the truly human in it, that he becomes accustomed to experiencing himself as a human being.... If man is unfree in the materialist sense – that is, is free not by reason of the negative force of being able to avoid this or that, but by reason of the positive power to assert his true individuality, then one should not punish individuals for crimes, but rather destroy the anti-social breeding places of crime.... If man is moulded by circumstances, then the circumstances must be moulded humanly" (see *Ludwig Feuerbach*, Appendix: "Karl Marx on the History of French Materialism of the XVIII Century"). [5]

Such is the second practical conclusion to be drawn from the materialist theory.

* * *

What is the anarchist view of the materialist theory of Marx and Engels?

While the dialectical method originated with Hegel, the materialist theory is a further development of the materialism of Feuerbach. The Anarchists know this very well, and they try to take advantage of the defects of Hegel and Feuerbach to discredit the dialectical materialism of Marx and Engels. We have already shown with reference to Hegel and the dialectical method that these tricks of the Anarchists prove nothing but their own ignorance. The same must be said with reference to their attacks on Feuerbach and the materialist theory.

For example. The Anarchists tell us with great aplomb that "Feuerbach was a pantheist..." that he "deified man..." (see *Nobati*, No. 7. D. Delendi), that "in Feuerbach's opinion man is what he eats..." alleging that from this Marx drew the following conclusion: "Consequently, the main and primary thing is economic conditions..." (see *Nobati*, No. 6, Sh. G.).

True, nobody has any doubts about Feuerbach's pantheism, his deification of man, and other errors of his of the same kind. On the contrary, Marx and Engels were the first to reveal Feuerbach's errors. Nevertheless, the Anarchists deem it necessary once again to "expose" the already exposed errors. Why? Probably because, in reviling Feuerbach, they want indirectly to discredit the materialist theory of Marx and Engels. Of course, if we examine the subject impartially we shall certainly find that in addition to erroneous ideas, Feuerbach gave utterance to correct ideas, as has been the case with many scholars in history. Nevertheless, the Anarchists go on "exposing."...

We say again that by tricks of this kind they prove nothing but their own ignorance.

It is interesting to note (as we shall see later on) that the Anarchists took it into their heads to criticise the materialist theory from hearsay, without any acquaintance with it. As a consequence, they often contradict and refute each other, which, of course, makes our "critics" look ridiculous. If, for example, we listen to what Mr. Cherkezishvili has to say, it

would appear that Marx and Engels detested monistic materialism, that their materialism was vulgar and not monistic materialism:

"The great science of the naturalists, with its system of evolution, transformism and monistic materialism, which *Engels so
heartily detested*... avoided dialectics," etc. (see *Nobati*, No. 4.
V. Cherkezishvili).

It follows, therefore, that natural-scientific materialism,
which Cherkezishvili approves of and which Engels "detested,"
was monistic materialism and, *therefore*, deserves approval,
whereas the materialism of Marx and Engels is not monistic
and, of course, does not deserve recognition.

Another Anarchist, however, says that the materialism of
Marx and Engels is monistic and *therefore* should be rejected.

"Marx's conception of history is a throwback to Hegel. The
monistic materialism of absolute objectivism in general, and
Marx's economic monism in particular, are impossible in nature
and fallacious in theory.... Monistic materialism is poorly disguised dualism and a compromise between metaphysics and
science..." (see *Nobati*, No. 6. Sh. G.).

It would follow, therefore, that monistic materialism is unacceptable, that Marx and Engels do not detest it, but, on the
contrary, are themselves monistic materialists – and therefore,
monistic materialism must be rejected.

They are all at sixes and sevens. Try and make out which of
them is right, the former or the latter! They have not yet agreed
among themselves about the merits and demerits of Marx's materialism, they have not yet understood whether it is monistic or
not, and have not yet made up their minds themselves as to
which is the more acceptable, vulgar or monistic materialism –
but they already deafen us with their boastful claims to have
shattered Marxism!

Well, well, if Messieurs the Anarchists continue to shatter each other's views as zealously as they are doing now, we need say no more, the future belongs to the Anarchists....

No less ridiculous is the fact that certain "celebrated" Anarchists, notwithstanding their "celebrity," have not yet made themselves familiar with the different trends in science. It appears that they are ignorant of the fact that there are various kinds of materialism in science which differ a great deal from each other: there is, for example, vulgar materialism, which denies the importance of the ideal side and the effect it has upon the material side; but there is also so-called monistic materialism – the materialist theory of Marx – which scientifically examines the interrelation between the ideal and the material sides. But the Anarchists *confuse* these different kinds of materialism, fail to see even the obvious differences between them, and at the same time affirm with great aplomb that they are regenerating science!

P. Kropotkin, for example, smugly asserts in his "philosophical" works that anarcho-communism rests on "contemporary materialist philosophy," but he does not utter a single word to explain on which "materialist philosophy" anarcho-communism rests: on vulgar, monistic, or some other. Evidently he is ignorant of the fact that there are fundamental contradictions between the different trends of materialism, and he fails to understand that to confuse these trends means not "regenerating science," but displaying one's own downright ignorance (see Kropotkin, *Science and Anarchism*, and also *Anarchy and Its Philosophy*).

The same thing must be said about Kropotkin's Georgian disciples. Listen to this:

"In the opinion of Engels, and also of Kautsky, Marx rendered mankind a great service in that he..." among other things, discovered the "materialist conception. Is this true? We do not think so, for we know... that all the historians, scientists and

32

philosophers who adhere to the view that the social mechanism is set in motion by geographic, climatic and telluric, cosmic, anthropological and biological conditions – *are all materialists*" (see *Nobati*, No. 2).

It follows, therefore, that there is no difference whatever between the "materialism" of Aristotle and Holbach, or between the "materialism" of Marx and Moleschott! This is criticism if you like! And people whose knowledge is on such a level have taken it into their heads to renovate science! Indeed, it is an apt saying: "It's a bad lookout when a cobbler begins to bake pies!..."

To proceed. Our "celebrated" Anarchists heard somewhere that Marx's materialism was a "belly theory," and so they rebuke us, Marxists, saying:

"In the opinion of Feuerbach, man is what he eats. This formula had a magic effect on Marx and Engels," and, as a consequence, Marx drew the conclusion that "the main and primary thing is economic conditions, relations of production...." And then the Anarchists proceed to instruct us in a philosophical tone: "It would be a mistake to say that the *sole* means of achieving this object of social life) is *eating* and economic production.... If *ideology were determined* mainly, monistically, by *eating* and economic conditions – then some gluttons would be geniuses" (see *Nobati*, No. 6. Sh. G.).

You see how easy it is to refute the materialism of Marx and Engels! It is sufficient to hear some gossip in the street from some schoolgirl about Marx and Engels, it is sufficient to repeat that street gossip with philosophical aplomb in the columns of a paper like *Nobati*, to leap into fame as a "critic" of Marxism!

But tell me, gentlemen: Where, when, on which planet, and which Marx did you hear say that "*eating determines ideology*"? Why did you not cite a single sentence, a single word from the works of Marx to back your assertion? True, Marx said that the economic conditions of men determine their consciousness, their ideology, but who told you that eating and economic conditions are the same thing? Don't you really know that physiological phenomena, such as *eating*, for example, differ fundamentally from sociological phenomena, such as the *economic conditions* of men, for example? One can forgive a schoolgirl, say, for confusing these two different phenomena; but how is it that you, the "vanquishers of Social Democracy," "regenerators of science," so carelessly repeat the mistake of a schoolgirl?

How, indeed, can eating determine social ideology? Ponder over what you yourselves have said: eating, the form of eating, does not change; in ancient times people ate, masticated and digested their food in the same way as they do now, but ideology changes all the time. Ancient, feudal, bourgeois and proletarian – such are the forms of ideology. Is it conceivable that *that which does not change* can determine *that which is constantly changing*?

To proceed further. In the opinion of the Anarchists, Marx's materialism "is parallelism...." Or again: "monistic materialism is poorly disguised dualism and a compromise between metaphysics and science...." "Marx drops into dualism because he depicts relations of production as material, and human striving and will *as an illusion and a utopia*, which, even though it exists, *is of no importance*" (see *Nobati*, No. 6. Sh. G.).

Firstly, Marx's monistic materialism has nothing in common with silly parallelism. From the standpoint of this materialism, the material side, content, necessarily *precedes* the ideal side, form. Parallelism, however, repudiates this view and emphatically affirms that neither the material nor the ideal *comes first*, that both develop together, side by side.

Secondly, even if Marx had in fact "depicted relations of production as material, and human striving and will as an illusion and a utopia having no importance," does that mean that Marx was a dualist? The dualist, as is well known, ascribes *equal* importance to the ideal and material sides as two opposite principles. But if, as you say, Marx attaches higher importance to the material side and no importance to the ideal side because it is a "utopia," how do you make out that Marx was a dualist, Messieurs "Critics"?

Thirdly, what connection can there be between materialist monism and dualism, when even a child knows that monism springs from *one principle* – nature, or being, which has a material and an ideal form, whereas dualism springs from *two principles* – the material and the ideal, which, according to dualism, negate each other?

Fourthly, when did Marx depict "human striving and will as a utopia and an illusion"? True, Marx explained "human striving and will" by economic development, and when the strivings of certain armchair philosophers failed to harmonise with economic conditions he called them utopian. But does this mean that Marx believed that human striving in general is utopian? Does this, too, really need explanation? Have you really not read Marx's statement that: "*mankind always sets itself only such tasks as it can solve* " (see Preface to *A Contribution to the Critique of Political Economy*), i.e., that, generally speaking, mankind does not pursue utopian aims? Clearly, either our "critic" does not know what he is talking about, or he is deliberately distorting the facts.

Fifthly, who told you that in the opinion of Marx and Engels "human striving and will are of no importance"? Why do you not point to the place where they say that? Does not Marx speak of the importance of "striving and will" in his *Eighteenth Brumaire of Louis Bonaparte*, in his *Class Struggles in France*, in his *Civil War in France*, and in other pamphlets of the same kind? Why then did Marx try to develop the proletarians' "will and striving" in the socialist spirit, why did he conduct propaganda among them if he attached no importance to "striving and will"? Or, what did Engels talk about in his well-known articles of 1891-94 if not the "importance of will and striving"? True, in Marx's opinion human "will and striving" acquire their content from economic conditions, but does that mean that they themselves exert no influence on the development of economic relations? Is it really so difficult for the Anarchists to understand such a simple idea?

Here is another "accusation" Messieurs the Anarchists make: "form is inconceivable without content..." therefore, one cannot say that "form *comes after* content (lags behind content. *K.*)... they 'co-exist.'... Otherwise, monism would be an absurdity" (see *Nobati*, No. 1. Sh. G.).

Our "scholar" is somewhat confused again. It is quite true that content is inconceivable without form. But it is also true that the *existing form* never fully corresponds to the *existing content*: the former lags behind the latter, to a certain extent the new content is always clothed in the old form and, as a consequence, there is always a conflict between the old form and the new content. It is precisely on this ground that revolutions occur, and this, among other things, expresses the revolutionary spirit of Marx's materialism. The "celebrated" Anarchists, however, have failed to understand this, and for this they themselves and not the materialist theory are to blame, of course.

Such are the views of the Anarchists on the materialist theory of Marx and Engels, that is, if they can be called views at all.

III

PROLETARIAN SOCIALISM

We are now familiar with Marx's theoretical doctrine; we are familiar with his *method* and also with his *theory*.

What practical conclusions must we draw from this doctrine?

What connection is there between dialectical materialism and proletarian socialism?

The dialectical method affirms that only that class which is growing day by day, which always marches forward and fights unceasingly for a better future, can be progressive to the end, only that class can smash the yoke of slavery. We see that the only class which is steadily growing, which always marches forward and is fighting for the future is the urban and rural proletariat. Therefore, we must serve the proletariat and place our hopes on it.

Such is the first practical conclusion to be drawn from Marx's theoretical doctrine.

But there is service and service. Bernstein also "serves" the proletariat when he urges it to forget about socialism. Kropotkin also "serves" the proletariat when he offers it community "socialism," which is scattered and has no broad industrial base. And Karl Marx serves the proletariat when he calls it to proletarian socialism, which will rest on the broad basis of modern large-scale industry.

What must we do in order that our activities may benefit the proletariat? How should we serve the proletariat?

The materialist theory affirms that a given ideal may be of direct service to the proletariat only if it does not run counter to the economic development of the country, if it fully answers to the requirements of that development. The economic development of the capitalist system shows that present-day production is assuming a social character, that the social character of production is a fundamental negation of existing capitalist property; consequently, our main task is to help to abolish capitalist property and to establish socialist property. And that means that the doctrine of Bernstein, who urges that socialism should be forgotten, fundamentally contradicts the requirements of economic development – it is harmful to the proletariat.

Further, the economic development of the capitalist system shows that present-day production is expanding day by day; it is not confined within the limits of individual towns and provinces, but constantly overflows these limits and embraces the territory of the whole state – consequently, we must welcome the expansion of production and regard as the basis of future socialism not separate towns and communities, but the entire and indivisible territory of the whole state which, in future, will, of course, expand more and more. And this means that the doctrine advocated by Kropotkin, which confines future socialism within the limits of separate towns and communities, is contrary to the interests of a powerful expansion of production – it is harmful to the proletariat.

Fight for a *broad* socialist life as the *principal* goal – this is how we should serve the proletariat.

Such is the second practical conclusion to be drawn from Marx's theoretical doctrine.

Clearly, proletarian socialism is the logical deduction from dialectical materialism.

What is proletarian socialism?

The present system is a capitalist system. This means that the world is divided up into two opposing camps, the camp of a small handful of capitalists and the camp of the majority – the proletarians. The proletarians work day and night, nevertheless they remain poor. The capitalists do not work, nevertheless they are rich. This takes place not because the proletarians are unintelligent and the capitalists are geniuses, but because the capitalists appropriate the fruits of the labour of the proletarians, because the capitalists exploit the proletarians.

Why are the fruits of the labour of the proletarians appropriated by the capitalists and not by the proletarians? Why do the capitalists exploit the proletarians and not vice versa?

Because the capitalist system is based on commodity production: here everything assumes the form of a commodity, everywhere the principle of buying and selling prevails. Here you can buy not only articles of consumption, not only food products, but also the labour power of men, their blood and their consciences. The capitalists know all this and purchase the labour power of the proletarians, they hire them. This means that the capitalists become the owners of the labour power they buy. The proletarians, however, lose their right to the labour power which they have sold. That is to say, what is produced by that labour power no longer belongs to the proletarians, it belongs only to the capitalists and goes into their pockets. The labour power which you have sold may produce in the course of a day goods to the value of 100 rubles, but that is not your business, those goods do not belong to you, it is the business only of the capitalists, and the goods belong to them – all that you are due to receive is your daily wage which, perhaps, may be sufficient to satisfy your essential needs if, of course, you live frugally. Briefly: the capitalists buy the labour power of the proletarians, they hire the proletarians, and this is precisely why the capitalists appropriate the fruits of the labour of the proletarians, this is precisely why the capitalists exploit the proletarians and not vice versa.

But why is it precisely the capitalists who buy the labour power of the proletarians? Why do the capitalists hire the proletarians and not vice versa?

Because the principal basis of the capitalist system is the private ownership of the instruments and means of production. Because the factories, mills, the land and minerals, the forests, the railways, machines and other means of production have become the private property of a small handful of capitalists. Because the proletarians lack all this. That is why the capitalists hire proletarians to keep the factories and mills going – if they did not do that their instruments and means of production would yield no profit. That is why the proletarians sell their labour power to the capitalists – if they did not, they would die of starvation.

All this throws light on the general character of capitalist production. Firstly, it is self-evident that capitalist production cannot be united and organised: it is all split up among the private enterprises of individual capitalists. Secondly, it is also clear that the immediate purpose of this scattered production is not to satisfy the needs of the people, but to produce goods for sale in order to increase the profits of the capitalists. But as every capitalist strives to increase his profits, each one tries to produce the largest possible quantity of goods and, as a result, the market is soon glutted, prices fall and – a general crisis sets in.

Thus, crises, unemployment, suspension of production, anarchy of production, and the like, are the direct results of present-day unorganised capitalist production.

If this unorganised social system still remains standing, if it still firmly withstands the attacks of the proletariat, it is primarily because it is protected by the capitalist state, by the capitalist government.

Such is the basis of present-day capitalist society.

* * *

There can be no doubt that future society will be built on an entirely different basis.

Future society will be socialist society. This means primarily, that there will be no classes in that society; there will be neither capitalists nor proletarians and, consequently, there will be no exploitation. In that society there will be only workers engaged in collective labour.

Future society will be socialist society. This means also that, with the abolition of exploitation commodity production and buying and selling will also be abolished and, therefore, there will be no room for buyers and sellers of labour power, for employers and employed – there will be only free workers.

Future society will be socialist society. This means, lastly, that in that society the abolition of wage-labour will be accompanied by the complete abolition of the private ownership of the instruments and means of production; there will be neither poor proletarians nor rich capitalists – there will be only workers who collectively own all the land and minerals, all the forests, all the factories and mills, all the railways, etc.

As you see, the main purpose of production in the future will be to satisfy the needs of society and not to produce goods for sale in order to increase the profits of the capitalists. Where there will be no room for commodity production, struggle for profits, etc.

It is also clear that future production will be socialistically organised, highly developed production, which will take into account the needs of society and will produce as much as society needs. Here there will be no room whether for scattered production, competition, crises, or unemployment.

Where there are no classes, where there are neither rich nor poor, there is no need for a state, there is no need either for political power, which oppresses the poor and protects the rich. Consequently, in socialist society there will be no need for the existence of political power.

That is why Karl Marx said as far back as 1846:

"The working class in the course of its development will substitute for the old bourgeois society an *association* which will exclude classes and their antagonism, and there will be *no more political power properly so-called...*" (see *The Poverty of Philosophy*).[6]

That is why Engels said in 1884:

"The state, then, has not existed from all eternity. There have been societies that did without it, that had no conception of the state and state power. At a certain stage of economic development, which was necessarily bound up with the cleavage of society into classes, the state became a necessity.... We are now rapidly approaching a stage in the development of production at which the existence of these classes not only will have ceased to be a necessity, but will become a positive hindrance to production. They will fall as inevitably as they arose at an earlier stage. *Along with them the state will inevitably fall.* The society that will organise production on the basis of a free and equal association of the producers will put the whole machinery of state where it will then belong: into the Museum of Antiquities, by the side of the spinning wheel and the bronze axe" (see *The Origin of the Family, Private Property and the State*).[7]

At the same time, it is self-evident that for the purpose of administering public affairs there will have to be in socialist society, in addition to local offices which will collect all sorts of information, a central statistical bureau, which will collect information about the needs of the whole of society, and then distribute the various kinds of work among the working people accordingly. It will also be necessary to hold conferences, and particularly congresses, the decisions of which will certainly be binding upon the comrades in the minority until the next congress is held.

Lastly, it is obvious that free and comradely labour should result in an equally comradely, and complete, satisfaction of all needs in the future socialist society This means that if future society demands from each of its members as much labour as he can perform, it, in its turn, must provide each member with all the products he needs. From each according to his ability, to each according to his needs! – such is the basis upon which the future collectivist system must be created. It goes without saying that in the *first* stage of socialism, when elements who have not yet grown accustomed to work are being drawn into the new way of life, when the productive forces also will not yet have been sufficiently developed and there will still be "dirty" and "clean" work to do, the application of the principle: "to each according to his needs," will undoubtedly be greatly hindered and, as a consequence, society will be obliged *temporarily* to take some other path, a middle path. But it is also clear that when future society runs into its groove, when the survivals of capitalism will have been eradicated, the only principle that will conform to socialist society will be the one pointed out above.

That is why Marx said in 1875:

"In a higher phase of communist (i.e., socialist) society, after the enslaving subordination of the individual to the division of labour, and therewith also the antithesis between mental and physical labour, has vanished; after labour has become not only a means of livelihood but life's prime want; after the productive forces have also increased with the all-round development of the individual... only then can the narrow horizon of bourgeois law be crossed in its entirety and society inscribe on its banners: 'From each according to his ability, to each according to his needs'" (see *Critique of the Gotha Programme*).[8]

Such, in general, is the picture of future socialist society according to the theory of Marx.

This is all very well. But is the achievement of socialism conceivable? Can we assume that man will rid himself of his "savage habits"?

Or again: if everybody receives according to his needs, can we assume that the level of the productive forces of socialist society will be adequate for this?

Socialist society presupposes an adequate development of productive forces and socialist consciousness among men, their socialist enlightenment. At the present time the development of productive forces is hindered by the existence of capitalist property, but if we bear in mind that this capitalist property will not exist in future society, it is self-evident that the productive forces will increase tenfold. Nor must it be forgotten that in future society the hundreds of thousands of present-day parasites, and also the unemployed, will set to work and augment the ranks of the working people; and this will greatly stimulate the development of the productive forces. As regards men's "savage" sentiments and opinions, these are not as eternal as some people imagine; there was a time, under primitive communism, when man did not recognise private property; there came a time, the time of individualistic production, when private property dominated the hearts and minds of men; a new time is coming, the time of socialist production – will it be surprising if the hearts and minds of men become imbued with socialist strivings? Does not being determine the "sentiments" and opinions of men?

But what proof is there that the establishment of the socialist system is inevitable? Must the development of modern capitalism inevitably be followed by socialism? Or, in other words: How do we know that Marx's proletarian socialism is not merely a sentimental dream, a fantasy? Where is the scientific proof that it is not?

History shows that the form of property is directly determined by the form of production and, as a consequence, a change in the form of production is sooner or later inevitably followed by a change in the form of property. There was a time when property bore a communistic character, when the forests and fields in which primitive men roamed belonged to all and not to individuals. Why did communist property exist at that time? Because production was communistic, labour was performed in common, collectively – all worked together and could not dispense with each other. A different period set in, the period of petty-bourgeois production, when property assumed an individualistic (private) character, when everything that man needed (with the exception, of course, of air, sunlight, etc.) was regarded as private property. Why did this change take place? Because production became individualistic; each one began to work for himself, stuck in his own little corner. Finally there came a time, the time of large-scale capitalist production, when hundreds and thousands of workers gather under one roof, in one factory, and engage in collective labour. Here you do not see the old method of working individually, each pulling his own way – here every worker is closely associated in his work with his comrades in his own shop, and all of them are associated with the other shops. It is sufficient for one shop to stop work for the workers in the entire plant to become idle. As you see, the process of production, labour, has already assumed a social character, has acquired a socialist hue. And this takes place not only in individual factories, but in entire branches of industry, and between branches of industry; it is sufficient for the railwaymen to go on strike for production to be put in difficulties, it is sufficient for the production of oil and coal to come to a standstill for whole factories and mills to close down after a time. Clearly, here the process of production has assumed a social, collective character. As, however, the private character of appropriation does not correspond to the social character of production, as present-day collective labour must inevitably lead to collective property, it is self-evident that the socialist system will follow capitalism as inevitably as day follows night.

That is how history proves the inevitability of Marx's proletarian socialism.

* * *

History teaches us that the class or social group which plays the principal role in social production and performs the main functions in production must, in the course of time, inevitably take control of that production. There was a time, under the matriarchate, when women were regarded as the masters of production. Why was this? Because under the kind of production then prevailing, primitive agriculture, women played the principal role in production, they performed the main functions, while the men roamed the forests in quest of game. Then came the time, under the patriarchate, when the predominant position in production passed to men. Why did this change take place? Because under the kind of production prevailing at that time, stock-raising, in which the principal instruments of production were the spear, the lasso and the bow and arrow, the principal role was played by men.... There came the time of large-scale capitalist production, in which the proletarians begin to play the principal role in production, when all the principal functions in production pass to them, when without them production cannot go on for a single day (let us recall general strikes), and when the capitalists, far from being needed for production, are even a hindrance to it. What does this signify? It signifies either that all social life must collapse entirely, or that the proletariat, sooner or later, but inevitably, must take control of modern production, must become its sole owner, its socialistic owner.

Modern industrial crises, which sound the death knell of capitalist property and bluntly put the question: capitalism *or* socialism, make this conclusion absolutely obvious; they vividly reveal the parasitism of the capitalists and the inevitability of the victory of socialism.

That is how history further proves the inevitability of Marx's proletarian socialism.

Proletarian socialism is based not on sentiment, not on abstract "justice," not on love for the proletariat, but on the scientific grounds referred to above.

That is why proletarian socialism is also called "scientific socialism."

Engels said as far back as 1877:

"If for the imminent overthrow of the present mode of distribution of the products of labour... we had no better guarantee than the consciousness that this mode of distribution is unjust, and that justice must eventually triumph, we should be in a pretty bad way, and we might have a long time to wait...." The most important thing in this is that "the productive forces created by the modern capitalist mode of production and the system of distribution of goods established by it have come into crying contradiction with that mode of production itself, and in fact to such a degree that, if the whole of modern society is not to perish, a revolution of the mode of production and distribution must take place, a revolution which will put an end to all class divisions. On this tangible, material fact... and not on the conceptions of justice and injustice held by any armchair philosopher, is modern socialism's confidence of victory founded" (see *Anti-Dühring*).[9]

That does not mean, of course, that since capitalism is decaying the socialist system can be established any time we like. Only Anarchists and other petty-bourgeois ideologists think that. The socialist ideal is not the ideal of all classes. It is the ideal only of the proletariat; not all classes are directly interested in its fulfilment, the proletariat alone is so interested. This means that as long as the proletariat constitutes a small section of society the establishment of the socialist system is impossible. The decay of the old form of production, the further concentration of capitalist production, and the proletarianisation of the majority in society – such are the conditions needed for the achievement of socialism. But this is still not enough. The majority in society may already be proletarianised, but socialism may still not be achievable. This is because, in addition to all this, the achievement of socialism calls for class consciousness, the unity of the proletariat and the ability of the proletariat to manage its own affairs. In order that all this may be acquired, what is called political freedom is needed, i.e., freedom of speech, press, strikes and association, in short, freedom to wage the class struggle. But political freedom is not equally ensured everywhere. Therefore, the conditions under which it is obliged to wage the struggle: under a feudal autocracy (Russia), a constitutional monarchy (Germany), a big bourgeois republic (France), or under a democratic republic (which Russian Social-Democracy is demanding), are not a matter of indifference to the proletariat. Political freedom is best and most fully ensured in a democratic republic, that is, of course, in so far as it can be ensured under capitalism at all. Therefore, all advocates of proletarian socialism necessarily strive for the establishment of a democratic republic as the best "bridge" to socialism.

That is why, under present conditions, the Marxist programme is divided into two parts: the *maximum programme*, the goal of which is socialism, and the *minimum programme*, the object of which is to lay the road to socialism through a democratic republic.

* * *

What must the proletariat do, what path must it take in order consciously to carry out its programme, to overthrow capitalism and build socialism?

The answer is clear: the proletariat cannot achieve socialism by making peace with the bourgeoisie – it must unfailingly take the path of struggle, and this struggle must be a class struggle, a struggle of the entire proletariat against the entire bourgeoisie. Either the bourgeoisie and its capitalism, or the proletariat and its socialism! That must be the basis of the proletariat's actions, of its class struggle.

But the proletarian class struggle assumes numerous forms. A strike, for example – whether partial or general makes no difference – is class struggle. Boycott and sabotage are undoubtedly class struggle. Meetings, demonstrations, activity in public representative bodies, etc. – whether national parliaments or local government bodies makes no difference – are also class struggle. All these are different forms of the same class struggle. We shall not here examine which form of struggle is more important for the proletariat in its class struggle, we shall merely observe that, in its proper time and place, each is undoubtedly needed by the proletariat as essential means for developing its class consciousness and organisation; and the proletariat needs class consciousness and organisation as much as it needs air. It must also be observed, however, that for the proletariat, all these forms of struggle are merely *preparatory* means, that not one of them, taken separately, constitutes the *decisive* means by which the proletariat can smash capitalism. Capitalism cannot be smashed by the general strike alone: the general strike can only create some of the conditions that are necessary for the smashing of capitalism. It is inconceivable that the proletariat should be able to overthrow capitalism merely by its activity in parliament: parliamentarism can only prepare some of the conditions that are necessary for overthrowing capitalism.

What, then, is the *decisive* means by which the proletariat will overthrow the capitalist system?

The *socialist revolution* is this means.

Strikes, boycott, parliamentarism, meetings and demonstrations are all good forms of struggle as means for preparing and organising the proletariat. But not one of these means is capable of abolishing existing inequality. All these means must be concentrated in one principal and decisive means; the proletariat must rise and launch a determined attack upon the bourgeoisie in order to destroy capitalism to its foundations. This principal and decisive means is the socialist revolution.

The socialist revolution must not be conceived as a sudden and short blow, it is a prolonged struggle waged by the proletarian masses, who inflict defeat upon the bourgeoisie and capture its positions. And as the victory of the proletariat will at the same time mean domination over the vanquished bourgeoisie, as, *in a collision of classes*, the defeat of one class signifies the domination of the other, the first stage of the socialist revolution will be the political domination of the proletariat over the bourgeoisie. The socialist *dictatorship of the proletariat*, capture of power by the proletariat – this is what the socialist revolution must start with.

This means that *until the bourgeoisie is completely vanquished*, until its wealth has been confiscated, the proletariat must without fail possess a military force, it must without fail have its "proletarian guard," with the aid of which it will repel the counter-revolutionary attacks of the dying bourgeoisie, exactly as the Paris proletariat did during the Commune.

The socialist dictatorship of the proletariat is needed to enable the proletariat to expropriate the bourgeoisie, to enable it to confiscate the land, forests, factories and mills, machines, railways, etc., from the entire bourgeoisie.

The expropriation of the bourgeoisie – this is what the socialist revolution must lead to.

This, then, is the principal and decisive means by which the proletariat will overthrow the present capitalist system.

That is why Karl Marx said as far back as 1847:

"...The first step in the revolution by the working class, is to raise the proletariat to the position of ruling class.... The proletariat will use its political supremacy to wrest, by degrees, all capital from the bourgeoisie, to centralise all instruments of production in the hands... of the proletariat organised as the ruling class..." (see the *Communist Manifesto*).

That is how the proletariat must proceed if it wants to bring about socialism.

From this general principle emerge all the other views on tactics. Strikes, boycott, demonstrations, and parliamentarism are important only in so far as they help to organise the proletariat and to strengthen and enlarge its organisations for accomplishing the socialist revolution.

* * *

Thus, to bring about socialism, the socialist revolution is needed, and the socialist revolution must begin with the dictatorship of the proletariat, i.e., the proletariat must capture political power as a means with which to expropriate the bourgeoisie.

But to achieve all this the proletariat must be organised, the proletarian ranks must be closely-knit and united, strong proletarian organisations must be formed, and these must steadily grow.

What forms must the proletarian organisations assume?

The most widespread, mass organisations are trade unions and workers' co-operatives (mainly producers' and consumers' co-operatives). The object of the trade unions is to fight (mainly) against industrial capital to improve the conditions of the workers within the limits of the present capitalist system. The object of the co-operatives is to fight (mainly) against merchant capital to secure an increase of consumption among the workers by reducing the prices of articles of prime necessity, also within the limits of the capitalist system, of course. The proletariat undoubtedly needs both trade unions and co-operatives as means of organising the proletarian masses. Hence, from the point of view of the proletarian socialism of Marx and Engels, the proletariat must utilise both these forms of organisation and reinforce and strengthen them, as far as this is possible under present political conditions, of course.

But trade unions and co-operatives alone cannot satisfy the organisational needs of the militant proletariat. This is because the organisations mentioned cannot go beyond the limits of capitalism, for their object is to improve the conditions of the workers under the capitalist system. The workers, however, want to free themselves entirely from capitalist slavery, they want to smash these limits, and not merely operate within the limits of capitalism. Hence, in addition, an organisation is needed that will rally around itself the class-conscious elements of the workers of *all* trades, that will transform the proletariat into a conscious class and make it its chief aim to smash the capitalist system, to prepare for the socialist revolution.

Such an organisation is the Social-Democratic Party of the proletariat.

This Party must be a class party, and it must be quite independent of other parties – and this is because it is the party of the proletarian class, the emancipation of which can be brought about only by this class itself.

This Party must be a revolutionary party – and this because the workers can be emancipated only by revolutionary means, by means of the socialist revolution.

This Party must be an international party, the doors of the Party must be open to all class-conscious proletarians – and this because the emancipation of the workers is not a national but a social question, equally important for the Georgian proletarians, for the Russian proletarians, and for the proletarians of other nations.

Hence, it is clear, that the more closely the proletarians of the different nations are united, the more thoroughly the national barriers which have been raised between them are demolished, the stronger will the Party of the proletariat be, and the more will the organisation of the proletariat in one indivisible class be facilitated.

Hence, it is necessary, as far as possible, to introduce the principle of centralism in the proletarian organisations as against the looseness of federation – irrespective of whether these organisations are party, trade union or co-operative.

It is also clear that all these organisations must be built on a democratic basis, in so far as this is not hindered by political or other conditions, of course.

What should be the relations between the Party on the one hand and the co-operatives and trade unions on the other? Should the latter be party or non-party? The answer to this question depends upon where and under what conditions the proletariat has to fight. At all events, there can be no doubt that the friendlier the trade unions and co-operatives are towards the socialist party of the proletariat, the more fully will both develop. And this is because both these economic organisations, if they are not closely connected with a strong socialist party, often become petty, allow narrow craft interests to obscure general class interests and thereby cause great harm to the proletariat. It is therefore necessary, in all cases, to ensure that the trade unions and co-operatives are under the ideological and political influence of the Party. Only if this is done will the organisations mentioned be transformed into a socialist school that will organise the proletariat – at present split up into separate groups – into a conscious class.

Such, in general, are the characteristic features of the proletarian socialism of Marx and Engels.

How do the Anarchists look upon proletarian socialism?

First of all we must know that proletarian socialism is not simply a philosophical doctrine. It is the doctrine of the proletarian masses, their banner; it is honoured and "revered" by the proletarians all over the world. Consequently, Marx and Engels are not simply the founders of a philosophical "school" – they are the living leaders of the living proletarian movement, which is growing and gaining strength every day. Whoever fights against this doctrine, whoever wants to "overthrow" it, must keep all this well in mind so as to avoid having his head cracked for nothing in an unequal struggle. Messieurs the Anarchists are well aware of this. That is why, in fighting Marx and Engels, they resort to a most unusual and, in its way, a new weapon.

What is this new weapon? A new investigation of capitalist production? A refutation of Marx's *Capital?* Of course not! Or perhaps, having armed themselves with "new facts" and the "inductive" method, they "scientifically" refute the "Bible" of Social-Democracy – the *Communist Manifesto* of Marx and Engels? Again no! Then what is this extraordinary weapon?

It is the accusation that Marx and Engels indulged in "plagiarism"! Would you believe it? It appears that Marx and Engels wrote nothing original, that scientific socialism is a pure fiction, because the *Communist Manifesto* of Marx and Engels was, from beginning to end, "stolen" from the *Manifesto* of Victor Considérant. This is quite ludicrous, of course, but V. Cherkezishvili, the "incomparable leader" of the Anarchists, relates this amusing story with such aplomb, and a certain Pierre Ramus, Cherkezishvili's foolish "apostle," and our home grown Anarchists repeat this "discovery" with such fervour, that it is worth while dealing at least briefly with this "story."

Listen to Cherkezishvili:

"The entire theoretical part of the *Communist Manifesto*, namely, the first and second chapters... are taken from V. Considérant. Consequently, the *Manifesto* of Marx and Engels – that Bible of legal revolutionary democracy – is nothing but a clumsy paraphrasing of V. Considérant's *Manifesto*. Marx and Engels not only appropriated the contents of Considérant's *Manifesto* but even... borrowed some of its chapter headings" (see the symposium of articles by Cherkezishvili, Ramus and Labriola, published in German under the title of *The Origin of the "Communist Manifesto*," p. 10).

This story is repeated by another Anarchist, P. Ramus:

"It can be emphatically asserted that their (Marx-Engels's) major work (the *Communist Manifesto*) is simply theft (a plagiary), shameless theft; they did not, however, copy it word for word as ordinary thieves do, but stole only the ideas and theories..." (*ibid.*, p. 4).

This is repeated by our Anarchists in *Nobati, Musha,*[10] *Khma,*[11] and other papers.

Thus it appears that scientific socialism and its theoretical principles were "stolen" from Considérant's *Manifesto*.

Are there any grounds for this assertion?

What was V. Considérant?

What was Karl Marx?

V. Considérant, who died in 1893, was a disciple of the utopian Fourier and remained an incorrigible *utopian*, who placed his hopes for the "salvation of France" on the *conciliation* of classes.

Karl Marx, who died in 1883, was a materialist, *an enemy of the utopians*. He regarded the development of the productive forces and the *struggle* between classes as the guarantee of the liberation of mankind.

Is there anything in common between them?

The *theoretical* basis of scientific socialism is the materialist theory of Marx and Engels. From the standpoint of this theory the development of social life is wholly determined by the development of the productive forces. If the feudal-landlord system was superseded by the bourgeois system, the "blame" for this rests upon the development of the productive forces, which made the rise of the bourgeois system inevitable. Or again: if the present bourgeois system will inevitably be superseded by the socialist system, it is because this is called for by the development of the modern productive forces. Hence the historical necessity of the destruction of capitalism and the establishment of socialism. Hence the Marxist proposition that we must seek our ideals in the history of the development of the productive forces and not in the minds of men.

Such is the theoretical basis of the *Communist Manifesto* of Marx and Engels (see the *Communist Manifesto*, Chapters I and II).

Does V. Considérant's *Democratic Manifesto* say anything of the kind? Did Considérant accept the materialist point of view?

We assert that neither Cherkezishvili, nor Ramus, nor our *Nobatists* quote *a single* statement, or *a single* word from Considérant's *Democratic Manifesto* which would confirm that Considérant was a materialist and based the evolution of social life upon the development of the productive forces. On the contrary, we know very well that Considérant is known in the history of socialism as an idealist utopian (see Paul Louis, *The History of Socialism in France*).

What, then, induces these queer "critics" to indulge in this idle chatter? Why do they undertake to criticise Marx and Engels when they are even unable to distinguish idealism from materialism? Is it only to amuse people?...

The *tactical* basis of scientific socialism is the doctrine of uncompromising class struggle, for this is the *best* weapon the proletariat possesses. The proletarian class struggle is the weapon by means of which the proletariat will capture political power and then expropriate the bourgeoisie in order to establish socialism.

Such is the *tactical* basis of scientific socialism as expounded in the *Manifesto* of Marx and Engels.

Is anything like this said in Considérant's *Democratic Manifesto*? Did Considérant regard the class struggle as the best weapon the proletariat possesses?

As is evident from the articles of Cherkezishvili and Ramus (see the above-mentioned symposium), there is not a word about this in Considérant's *Manifesto* – it merely notes the class struggle as a deplorable fact. As regards the class struggle as a means of smashing capitalism, Considérant spoke of it in his *Manifesto* as follows:

"Capital, labour and talent – such are the three basic elements of production, the three sources of wealth, the three wheels of the industrial mechanism.... The three classes which represent them have 'common interests'; their function is to make the machines work for the capitalists and for the people.... Before them... is the great goal of organising *the association of classes within the unity* of the nation..." (see K. Kautsky's pamphlet *The Communist Manifesto – A Plagiary*, p. 14, where this passage from Considérant's *Manifesto* is quoted).

All classes, unite! – this is the slogan that V. Considérant proclaimed in his *Democratic Manifesto*.

What is there in common between these tactics of class *conciliation* and the tactics of uncompromising class struggle advocated by Marx and Engels, whose resolute call was: *Proletarians of all countries, unite against all anti-proletarian classes*?

There is nothing in common between them, of course!

Why, then, do Messieurs Cherkezishvili and their foolish followers talk this rubbish? Do they think we are dead? Do they think we shall not drag them into the light of day?!

And lastly, there is one other interesting point. V. Considérant lived right up to 1893. He published his *Democratic Manifesto* in 1843. At the end of 1847 Marx and Engels wrote their *Communist Manifesto*. After that the *Manifesto* of Marx and Engels was published over and over again in all European languages. Everybody knows that the *Manifesto* of Marx and Engels was an epoch-making document. Nevertheless, *nowhere* did Considérant or his friends *ever* state during the lifetime of Marx and Engels that the latter had stolen "socialism" from Considérant's *Manifesto*. Is this not strange, reader?

What, then, impels the "inductive" upstarts – I beg your pardon, "scholars" – to talk this rubbish? In whose name are they speaking? Are they more familiar with Considérant's *Manifesto* than was Considérant himself? Or perhaps they think that V. Considérant and his supporters had not read the *Communist Manifesto*?

But enough.... Enough because the Anarchists themselves do not take seriously the Quixotic crusade launched by Ramus and Cherkezishvili: the inglorious end of this ridiculous crusade is too obvious to make it worthy of much attention....

Let us proceed to the actual criticism.

* * *

The Anarchists suffer from a certain ailment: they are very fond of "criticising" the parties of their opponents, but they do not take the trouble to make themselves in the least familiar with these parties. We have seen the Anarchists behave precisely in this way when "criticising" the dialectical method and the materialist theory of the Social-Democrats (see Chapters I and II). They behave in the same way when they deal with the theory of scientific socialism of the Social-Democrats.

Let us, for example, take the following fact. Who does not know that fundamental disagreements exist between the Socialist-Revolutionaries and the Social-Democrats? Who does not know that the former repudiate Marxism, the materialist theory of Marxism, its dialectical method, its programme and the class struggle – whereas the Social-Democrats take their stand entirely on Marxism? These fundamental disagreements must be self-evident to anybody who has heard anything, if only with half an ear, about the controversy between *Revolutsionnaya Rossiya* (the organ of the Socialist-Revolutionaries) and *Iskra* (the organ of the Social-Democrats). But what will you say about those "critics" who fail to see this difference between the two and shout that both the Socialist Revolutionaries and the

Social-Democrats are Marxists? Thus, for example, the Anarchists assert that both *Revolutsionnaya Rossiya* and *Iskra* are Marxist organs (see the Anarchists' symposium *Bread and Freedom*, p. 202).

That shows how "familiar" the Anarchists are with the principles of Social-Democracy!

After this, the soundness of their "scientific criticism" will be self-evident....

Let us examine this "criticism."

The Anarchists' principal "accusation" is that they do not regard the Social-Democrats as genuine Socialists – you are not Socialists, you are enemies of socialism, they keep on repeating.

This is what Kropotkin writes on this score:

"...We arrive at conclusions different from those arrived at by the majority of the Economists... of the Social-Democratic school.... We... arrive at free communism, whereas the majority of Socialists (meaning Social-Democrats too – *The Author*) arrive at state capitalism and collectivism (see Kropotkin, *Modern Science and Anarchism*, pp. 74-75).

What is this "state capitalism" and "collectivism" of the Social-Democrats?

This is what Kropotkin writes about it:

"The German Socialists say that all accumulated wealth must be concentrated in the hands of the state, which will place it at the disposal of workers' associations, organise production and exchange, and control the life and work of society" (see Kropotkin, *The Speeches of a Rebel*, p. 64).

And further:

"In their schemes... the collectivists commit... a double mistake. They want to abolish the capitalist system, but they preserve the two institutions which constitute the foundations of this system: representative government and wage-labour" (see *The Conquest of Bread*, p. 148).... "Collectivism, as is well known... preserves... wage-labour. Only... representative government... takes the place of the employer...." The representatives of this government "retain the right to utilise in the interests of all the surplus value obtained from production. Moreover, in this system a distinction is made... between the labour of the common labourer and that of the trained man: the labour of the unskilled worker, in the opinion of the collectivists, is *simple* labour, whereas the skilled craftsman, engineer, scientist and so forth perform what Marx calls *complex* labour and have the right to higher wages" (*ibid.*, p. 52). Thus, the workers will receive their necessary products not according to their needs, but "in proportion to the services they render society" (*ibid.*, p. 157).

The Georgian Anarchists say the same thing only with greater aplomb. Particularly outstanding among them for the recklessness of his statements is Mr. Baton. He writes:

"What is the collectivism of the Social-Democrats? Collectivism, or more correctly, state capitalism, is based on the following principle: each must work as much as he likes, or as much as the state determines, and receives in reward the value of his labour in the shape of goods...." Consequently, here "there is needed a legislative assembly... there is needed (also) an executive power, i.e., ministers, all sorts of administrators, gendarmes and spies and, perhaps, also troops, if there are too many discontented" (see *Nobati*, No. 5, pp. 68-69).

Such is the first "accusation" of Messieurs the Anarchists against Social-Democracy.

* * *

Thus, from the arguments of the Anarchists it follows that:

1. In the opinion of the Social-Democrats, socialist society is impossible without a government which, in the capacity of principal master, will hire workers and will certainly have "ministers... gendarmes and spies." 2. In socialist society, in the

opinion of the Social-Democrats, the distinction between "dirty" and "clean" work will be retained, the principle "to each according to his needs" will be rejected, and another principle will prevail, viz., "to each according to his services."

Those are the two points on which the Anarchists' "accusation" against Social-Democracy is based.

Has this "accusation" advanced by Messieurs the Anarchists any foundation?

We assert that everything the Anarchists say on this subject is either the result of stupidity, or it is despicable slander.

Here are the facts.

As far back as 1846 Karl Marx said: "The working class in the course of its development will substitute for the old bourgeois society an association which will exclude classes and their antagonism, and there will be *no more political power properly so-called...*" (see *Poverty of Philosophy*).

A year later Marx and Engels expressed the same idea in the *Communist Manifesto* (*Communist Manifesto*, Chapter II).

In 1877 Engels wrote: "The first act in which the state really comes forward as the representative of society as a whole – the taking possession of the means of production in the name of society – is at the same time its last independent act as a state. The interference of the state power in social relations becomes superfluous in one sphere after another, and then ceases of itself.... The state is not 'abolished,' it *withers away*" (*Anti-Dühring*).

In 1884 the same Engels wrote: "The state, then, has not existed from all eternity. There have been societies that did without it, that had no conception of the state.... At a certain stage of economic development, which was necessarily bound up with the cleavage of society into classes, the state became a necessity.... We are now rapidly approaching a stage in the development of production at which the existence of these classes not only will have ceased to be a necessity, but will become a positive hindrance to production. They will fall as inevitably as they arose at an earlier stage. *Along with them the state will inevitably fall.* The society that will organise production on the basis of a free and equal association of the producers will put the whole machinery of state where it will then belong: into the Museum of Antiquities, by the side of the spinning wheel and the bronze axe" (see *Origin of the Family, Private Property and the State*).

Engels said the same thing again in 1891 (see his Introduction to *The Civil War in France*).

As you see, in the opinion of the Social-Democrats, socialist society is a society in which there will be no room for the so-called state, political power, with its ministers, governors, gendarmes, police and soldiers. The last stage in the existence of the state will be the period of the socialist revolution, when the proletariat will capture political power and set up its own government (dictatorship) for the final abolition of the bourgeoisie. But when the bourgeoisie is abolished, when classes are abolished, when socialism becomes firmly established, there will be no need for any political power – and the so-called state will retire into the sphere of history.

As you see, the above-mentioned "accusation" of the Anarchists is mere tittle-tattle devoid of all foundation.

As regards the second point in the "accusation," Karl Marx says the following about it:

"In a higher phase of communist (i.e., socialist) society, after the enslaving subordination of the individual to the division of labour, and therewith also the *antithesis* between *mental* and *physical labour, has vanished*; after labour has become... life's prime want; after the productive forces have also increased with the all-round development of the individual... only then can the narrow horizon of bourgeois law be crossed in its entirety and society inscribe on its banners: '*From each according to his ability, to each according to his needs'" (Critique of the Gotha Programme).*

As you see, in Marx's opinion, the higher phase of communist (i.e., socialist) society will be a system under which the division of work into "dirty" and "clean," and the contradiction between mental and physical labour will be completely abolished, labour will be equal, and in society the genuine communist principle will prevail: from each according to his ability, to each according to his needs. Here there is no room for wage-labour.

Clearly this "accusation" is also devoid of all foundation.

One of two things: either Messieurs the Anarchists have never seen the above-mentioned works of Marx and Engels and indulge in "criticism" on the basis of hearsay, or they are familiar with the above-mentioned works of Marx and Engels and are deliberately lying.

Such is the fate of the first "accusation."

The second "accusation" of the Anarchists is that they deny that Social-Democracy is *revolutionary.* You are not revolutionaries, you repudiate violent revolution, you want to establish socialism only by means of ballot papers – Messieurs the Anarchists tell us.

Listen to this:

"...Social-Democrats... are fond of declaiming on the theme of 'revolution,' 'revolutionary struggle,' 'fighting with arms in hand.'... But if you, in the simplicity of your heart, ask them for arms, they will solemnly hand you a ballot paper to vote in elections...." They affirm that "the only expedient tactics befitting revolutionaries are peaceful and legal parliamentarism, with the oath of allegiance to capitalism, to established power and to the entire existing bourgeois system" (see symposium *Bread and Freedom*, pp. 21, 22-23).

The Georgian Anarchists say the same thing, with even greater aplomb, of course. Take, for example, Baton, who writes:

"The whole of Social-Democracy... openly asserts that fighting with the aid of rifles and weapons is a bourgeois method of revolution, and that only by means of ballot papers, only by means of general elections, can parties capture power, and then, by means of a parliamentary majority and legislation, reorganise society" (see *The Capture of Political Power*, pp. 3-4).

That is what Messieurs the Anarchists say about the Marxists.

Has this "accusation" any foundation?

We affirm that here, too, the Anarchists betray their ignorance and their passion for slander.

Here are the facts.

As far back as the end of 1847, Karl Marx and Frederick Engels wrote:

"The Communists disdain to conceal their views and aims. They openly declare that their *ends can be obtained only by the forcible overthrow* of all existing social conditions. Let the ruling classes tremble at a Communistic Revolution. The proletarians have nothing to lose but their chains. They have a world to win. *Working men of all countries, unite!*" (See the *Manifesto of the Communist Party*. In some of the legal editions several words have been omitted in the translation.)

In 1850, in anticipation of another outbreak in Germany, Karl Marx wrote to the German comrades of that time as follows:

"Arms and ammunition must not be surrendered on any pretext... the *workers* must... *organise themselves independently as a proletarian guard with commanders... and with a general staff....*" And this "you must keep in view during and after the impending insurrection" (see *The Cologne Trial*. Marx's Address to the Communists). [12]

In 1851-52 Karl Marx and Frederick Engels wrote:

"...The insurrectionary career once entered upon, *act with the greatest determination, and on the offensive*. The defensive is the death of every armed rising.... Surprise your antagonists while their forces are scattering, prepare new successes, however small, but daily... force your enemies to a retreat before they can collect their strength against you; in the words of Danton, the greatest master of revolutionary policy yet known: *de l'audace, de l'audace, encore de l'audace!*" (*Revolution and Counter-revolution in Germany*.)

We think that something more than "ballot papers" is meant here.

Lastly, recall the history of the Paris Commune, recall how peacefully the Commune acted, when it was content with the victory in Paris and refrained from attacking Versailles, that hotbed of counter-revolution. What do you think Marx said at that time? Did he call upon the Parisians to go to the ballot box? Did he express approval of the complacency of the Paris workers (the whole of Paris was in the hands of the workers), did he approve of the good nature they displayed towards the vanquished Versaillese? Listen to what Marx said:

"What elasticity, what historical initiative, what a capacity for sacrifice in these Parisians! After six months of hunger... they rise, beneath Prussian bayonets.... History has no like example of like greatness! If they are defeated only their 'good nature' will be to blame. *They should have marched at once on Versailles*, after first Vinoy and then the reactionary section of the Paris National Guard had themselves retreated. They missed their opportunity because of conscientious scruples. They did not want to *start a civil war*, as if that mischievous abortion Thiers had not already started the civil war with his attempt to disarm Paris!" (*Letters to Kugelmann*.)[13]

That is how Karl Marx and Frederick Engels thought and acted.

That is how the Social-Democrats think and act.

But the Anarchists go on repeating: Marx and Engels and their followers are interested only in ballot papers – they repudiate violent revolutionary action!

As you see, this "accusation" is also slander, which exposes the Anarchists' ignorance about the essence of Marxism.

Such is the fate of the second "accusation."

* * *

The third "accusation" of the Anarchists consists in denying that Social-Democracy is a popular movement, describing the Social-Democrats as bureaucrats, and affirming that the Social-Democratic plan for the dictatorship of the proletariat spells death to the revolution, and since the Social-Democrats stand for such a dictatorship they actually want to establish not the dictatorship of the proletariat, but their own dictatorship over the proletariat.

Listen to Mr. Kropotkin:

"We Anarchists have pronounced final sentence upon dictatorship.... We know that every dictatorship, no matter how honest its intentions, will lead to the death of the revolution. We know... that the idea of dictatorship is nothing more or less than the pernicious product of governmental fetishism which... has always striven to perpetuate slavery" (see Kropotkin, *The Speeches of a Rebel*, p. 131). The Social-Democrats not only recognise revolutionary dictatorship, they also "advocate dictatorship over the proletariat.... The workers are of interest to them only in so far as they are a disciplined army under their control.... Social-Democracy strives through the medium of the proletariat to capture the state machine" (see *Bread and Freedom*, pp. 62, 63).

The Georgian Anarchists say the same thing:

"The dictatorship of the proletariat in the direct sense of the term is utterly impossible, because the advocates of dictatorship are state men, and their dictatorship will be not the free activities of the entire proletariat, but the establishment at the head of society of the same representative government that exists today" (see Bâton, *The Capture of Political Power*, p. 45). The Social-Democrats stand for dictatorship not in order to facilitate the emancipation of the proletariat, but in order... "*by their own rule to establish a new slavery*" (see *Nobati*, No. 1, p. 5. Bâton).

Such is the third "accusation" of Messieurs the Anarchists. It requires no great effort to expose this, one of the regular slanders uttered by the Anarchists with the object of deceiving their readers.

We shall not analyse here the deeply mistaken view of Kropotkin, according to whom every dictatorship spells death to revolution. We shall discuss this later when we discuss the Anarchists' tactics. At present we shall touch upon only the "accusation" itself.

As far back as the end of 1847 Karl Marl and Frederick Engels said that to establish socialism the proletariat must achieve political dictatorship in order, with the aid of this dictatorship, to repel the counter-revolutionary attacks of the bourgeoisie and to take from it the means of production; that this dictatorship must be not the dictatorship of a few individuals, but the dictatorship of the entire proletariat as a class:

"The proletariat will use its political supremacy to wrest, by degrees, all capital from the bourgeoisie, to centralise all instruments of production in the hands... of the proletariat organised as the ruling class..." (see the *Communist Manifesto*).

That is to say, the dictatorship of the proletariat will be a dictatorship of the entire proletariat as a class over the bourgeoisie and not the domination of a few individuals over the proletariat.

Later they repeated this same idea in nearly all their other works, such as, for example, *The Eighteenth Brumaire of Louis Bonaparte*, *The Class Struggles in France*, *The Civil War in*

France, Revolution and Counter-revolution in Germany, Anti-Dühring, and other works.

But this is not all; to ascertain how Marx and Engels conceived of the dictatorship of the proletariat, to ascertain to what extent they regarded this dictatorship as possible, for all this it is very interesting to know their attitude towards the Paris Commune. The point is that the dictatorship of the proletariat is denounced not only by the Anarchists but also by the urban petty bourgeoisie, including all kinds of butchers and tavern-keepers – by all those whom Marx and Engels called philistines. This is what Engels said about the dictatorship of the proletariat, addressing such philistines:

"Of late, the German philistine has once more been filled with wholesome terror at the words: *Dictatorship of the Proletariat*. Well and good, gentlemen, do you want to know what this dictatorship looks like? Look at the Paris Commune. That was the Dictatorship of the Proletariat" (see *The Civil War in France*, Introduction by Engels). [14]

As you see, Engels conceived of the dictatorship of the proletariat in the shape of the Paris Commune.

Clearly, everybody who wants to know what the dictatorship of the proletariat is as conceived of by Marxists must study the Paris Commune. Let us then turn to the Paris Commune. If it turns out that the Paris Commune was indeed the dictatorship of a few individuals over the proletariat, then – down with Marxism, down with the dictatorship of the proletariat! But if we find that the Paris Commune was indeed the dictatorship of the proletariat over the bourgeoisie, then... we shall laugh heartily at the anarchist slanderers who in their struggle against the Marxists have no alternative but to invent slander.

The history of the Paris Commune can be divided into two periods: the first period, when affairs in Paris were controlled by the well-known "Central Committee," and the second period, when, after the authority of the "Central Committee" had expired, control of affairs was transferred to the recently elected Commune. What was this "Central Committee," what was its composition? Before us lies Arthur Arnould's *Popular History of the Paris Commune* which, according to Arnould, briefly answers this question. The struggle had only just commenced when about 300,000 Paris workers, organised in companies and battalions, elected delegates from their ranks. In this way the "Central Committee" was formed.

"All these citizens (members of the "Central Committee") elected during partial elections by their companies or battalions," says Arnould, "were known only to the small groups whose delegates they were. Who were these people, what kind of people were they, and what did they want to do?" This was "an anonymous government consisting almost exclusively of common workers and minor office employees, the names of three fourths of whom were unknown outside their streets or offices.... Tradition was upset. Something unexpected had happened in the world. There was not a single member of the ruling classes among them. A revolution had broken out which was not represented by a single *lawyer*, *deputy*, *journalist* or *general*. Instead, there was a *miner* from Creusot, a *bookbinder*, a *cook*, and so forth" (see *A Popular History of the Paris Commune*, p. 107).

Arthur Arnould goes on to say:

"The members of the 'Central Committee' said: 'We are obscure bodies, humble tools of the attacked people.... Instruments of the people's will, we are here to be its echo, to achieve its triumph. The people want a Commune, and we shall remain in order to proceed to the election of the Commune.' Neither more nor less. These dictators do not put themselves above nor stand aloof from the masses. One feels that they are living with the masses, in the masses, by means of the masses, that they consult with them every second, that they listen and convey all they hear, striving only, in a concise form... to convey the opinion of three hundred thousand men" (*ibid.*, p. 109).

That is how the Paris Commune behaved in the first period of its existence.

Such was the Paris Commune.

Such is the dictatorship of the proletariat.

Let us now pass to the second period of the Commune, when the Commune functioned in place of the "Central Committee." Speaking of these two periods, which lasted two months, Arnould exclaims with enthusiasm that this was a real dictatorship of the people. Listen:

"The magnificent spectacle which this people presented during those two months imbues us with strength and hope ... to look into the face of the future. During those two months there was a real dictatorship in Paris, a most complete and uncontested dictatorship not of one man, *but of the entire people* – the sole master of the situation.... This dictatorship lasted uninterruptedly for over two months, from March 18 to May 22 (1871)...." In itself "... the Commune was only a moral power and possessed no other material strength than the universal sympathy... of the citizens, *the people were the rulers*, the only rulers, they themselves set up their police and magistracy..." (*ibid.*, pp. 242, 244).

That is how the Paris Commune is described by *Arthur Arnould*, a member of the Commune and an active participant in its hand-to-hand fighting.

The Paris Commune is described in the same way by another of its members and equally active participant *Lissagaray* (see his *History of the Paris Commune*).

The people as the "only rulers," "not the dictatorship of one man, but of the whole people" – this is what the Paris Commune was.

"Look at the Paris Commune. That was the dictatorship of the proletariat" – exclaimed Engels for the information of philistines.

So this is the dictatorship of the proletariat as conceived of by Marx and Engels.

As you see, Messieurs the Anarchists know as much about the dictatorship of the proletariat, the Paris Commune, and Marxism, which they so often "criticise," as you and I, dear reader, know about the Chinese language.

Clearly, there are two kinds of dictatorship. There is the dictatorship of the minority, the dictatorship of a small group, the dictatorship of the Trepovs and Ignatyevs, which is directed against the people. This kind of dictatorship is usually headed by a camarilla which adopts secret decisions and tightens the noose around the neck of the majority of the people.

Marxists are the enemies of such a dictatorship, and they fight such a dictatorship far more stubbornly and self-sacrificingly than do our noisy Anarchists.

There is another kind of dictatorship, the dictatorship of the proletarian majority, the dictatorship of the masses, which is directed against the bourgeoisie, against the minority. At the head of this dictatorship stand the masses; here there is no room either for a camarilla or for secret decisions, here everything is done openly, in the streets, at meetings – because it is the dictatorship of the street, of the masses, a dictatorship directed against all oppressors.

Marxists support this kind of dictatorship "with both hands" – and that is because such a dictatorship is the magnificent beginning of the great socialist revolution.

Messieurs the Anarchists confused these two mutually negating dictatorships and thereby put themselves in a ridiculous position: they are fighting not Marxism but the figments of their own imagination, they are fighting not Marx and Engels but windmills, as Don Quixote of blessed memory did in his day....

Such is the fate of the third "accusation."

(TO BE CONTINUED) [*]

Akhali Droyeba (*New Times*),
Nos. 5, 6, 7 and 8,
December 11, 18, 25, 1906
and January 1, 1907
Chveni Tskhovreba (*Our Life*),
Nos. 3, 5, 8 and 9,
February 21, 23, 27 and 28, 1907
Dro (*Time*) Nos. 21, 22, 23 and 26,
April 4, 5, 6 and 10, 1907

Signed: *Ko....*

Translated from the Georgian

---

[*] The continuation did not appear in the press because, in the middle of 1907, Comrade Stalin was transferred by the Central Committee of the Party to Baku for Party work, and several months later he was arrested there. His notes on the last chapters of his work *Anarchism or Socialism?* were lost when the police searched his lodgings. – *Ed.*

APPENDIX

ANARCHISM OR SOCIALISM?

DIALECTICAL MATERIALISM

I

We are not the kind of people who, when the word "anarchism" is mentioned, turn away contemptuously and say with a supercilious wave of the hand: "Why waste time on that, it's not worth talking about!" We think that such cheap "criticism" is undignified and useless.

Nor are we the kind of people who console themselves with the thought that the Anarchists "have no masses behind them and, therefore, are not so dangerous." It is not who has a larger or smaller "mass" following today, but the essence of the doctrine that matters. If the "doctrine" of the Anarchists expresses the truth, then it goes without saying that it will certainly hew a path for itself and will rally the masses around itself. If, however, it is unsound and built up on a false foundation, it will not last long and will remain suspended in mid-air. But the unsoundness of anarchism must be proved.

We believe that the Anarchists are real enemies of Marxism. Accordingly, we also hold that a real struggle must be waged against real enemies. Therefore, it is necessary to examine the "doctrine" of the Anarchists from beginning to end and weigh it up thoroughly from all aspects.

But in addition to criticising anarchism we must explain our own position and in that way expound in general outline the doctrine of Marx and Engels. This is all the more necessary for the reason that some Anarchists are spreading false conceptions about Marxism and are causing confusion in the minds of readers.

And so, let us proceed with our subject.

Everything in the world is in motion.... Life changes, productive forces grow, old relations collapse.... Eternal motion and eternal destruction and creation – such is the essence of life.

Karl Marx

(See *The Poverty of Philosophy*)

Marxism is not only the theory of socialism, it is an integral world outlook, a philosophical system, from which Marx's proletarian socialism logically follows. This philosophical system is called dialectical materialism. Clearly, to expound Marxism means to expound also dialectical materialism.

Why is this system called dialectical materialism?

Because its *method* is dialectical, and its *theory* is materialistic.

What is the dialectical method?

What is the materialist theory?

It is said that life consists in constant growth and development. And that is true: social life is not something immutable and static, it never remains at one level, it is in eternal motion, in an eternal process of destruction and creation. It was with good reason that Marx said that eternal motion and eternal destruction and creation are the essence of life. Therefore, life always contains the *new* and the *old*, the growing and the dying, revolution and reaction – in it something is always dying, and at the same time something is always being born....

The dialectical method tells us that we must regard life as it actually is. Life is in continual motion, and therefore life must be viewed in its motion, in its destruction and creation. Where is life going, what is dying and what is being born in life, what is being destroyed and what is being created? – these are the questions that should interest us first of all.

Such is the first conclusion of the dialectical method.

That which in life is born and grows day by day is invincible, its progress cannot be checked, its victory is inevitable. That is to say, if, for example, in life the proletariat is born and grows day by

74

day, no matter how weak and small in numbers it may be today, in the long run it must triumph. On the other hand, that which in life is dying and moving towards its grave must inevitably suffer defeat, i.e., if, for example, the bourgeoisie is losing ground and is slipping farther and farther back every day, then, no matter how strong and numerous it may be today, it must, in the long run, suffer defeat and go to its grave. Hence arose the well-known dialectical proposition: all that which really exists, i.e., all that which grows day by day is rational.

Such is the second conclusion of the dialectical method.

In the eighties of the nineteenth century a famous controversy flared up among the Russian revolutionary intelligentsia. The Narodniks asserted that the main force that could undertake the task of "emancipating Russia" was the poor peasantry. Why? – the Marxists asked them. Because, answered the Narodniks, the peasantry is the most numerous and at the same time the poorest section of Russian society. To this the Marxists replied: It is true that today the peasantry constitutes the majority and that it is very poor, but is that the point? The peasantry has long constituted the majority, but up to now it has displayed no initiative in the struggle for "freedom" without the assistance of the proletariat. Why? Because the peasantry as a class is *disintegrating day by day*, it is breaking up into the proletariat and the bourgeoisie, whereas the proletariat as a class *is day by day growing* and gaining strength. Nor is poverty of decisive importance here: tramps are poorer than the peasants, but nobody will say that they can undertake the task of "emancipating Russia." The only thing that matters is: Who is growing and who is becoming aged in life? As the proletariat is the only class which is steadily growing and gaining strength, our duty is to take our place by its side and recognise it as the main force in the Russian revolution – that is how the Marxists answered. As you see, the Marxists looked at the question from the dialectical standpoint, whereas the Narodniks argued metaphysically, because they regarded the phenomena of life as "immutable, static, given once and for all" (see F. Engels, *Philosophy, Political Economy, Socialism*).

That is how the dialectical method looks upon the movement of life.

But there is movement and movement. There was social movement in the "December days" when the proletariat, straightening its back, stormed arms depots and launched an attack upon reaction. But the movement of preceding years, when the proletariat, under the conditions of "peaceful" development, limited itself to individual strikes and the formation of small trade unions, must also be called social movement. Clearly, movement assumes different forms. And so the dialectical method says that movement has two forms: the evolutionary and the revolutionary form. Movement is evolutionary when the progressive elements spontaneously continue their daily activities and introduce minor *quantitative* changes in the old order. Movement is revolutionary when the same elements combine, become imbued with a single idea and sweep down upon the enemy camp with the object of uprooting the old order and its *qualitative* features and to establish a new order. Evolution prepares for revolution and creates the ground for it; revolution consummates the process of evolution and facilitates its further activity.

Similar processes take place in nature. The history of science shows that the dialectical method is a truly scientific method: from astronomy to sociology, in every field we find confirmation of the idea that nothing is eternal in the universe, everything changes, everything develops. Consequently, everything in nature must be regarded from the point of view of movement, development. And this means that the spirit of dialectics permeates the whole of present-day science.

As regards the forms of movement, as regards the fact that according to dialectics, minor, *quantitative* changes sooner or later lead to major, *qualitative* changes – this law applies with equal force to the history of nature. Mendeleyev's "periodic system of elements" clearly shows how very important in the history of nature is the emergence of qualitative changes out of quantitative changes. The same thing is shown in biology by the theory of neo-Lamarckism, to which neo-Darwinism is yielding place.

We shall say nothing about other facts, on which F. Engels has thrown sufficiently full light in his *Anti-Dühring*.

* * *

Thus, we are now familiar with the dialectical method. We know that according to that method the universe is in eternal motion, in an eternal process of destruction and creation, and that, consequently, all phenomena in nature and in society must be viewed in motion, in process of destruction and creation and not as something static and immobile. We also know that this motion has two forms: evolutionary and revolutionary....

How do our Anarchists look upon the dialectical method?

Everybody knows that Hegel was the father of the dialectical method. Marx merely purged and improved this method. The Anarchists are aware of this; they also know that Hegel was a conservative, and so, taking advantage of the "opportunity," they vehemently revile Hegel, throw mud at him as a "reactionary, as a supporter of restoration, and zealously try to "prove" that "Hegel... is a philosopher of restoration... that he eulogizes bureaucratic constitutionalism in its absolute form, that the general idea of his philosophy of history is subordinate to and serves the philosophical trend of the period of restoration," and so on and so forth (see *Nobati*, No. 6. Article by V. Cherkezishvili). True, nobody contests what they say on this point; on the contrary, everybody agrees that Hegel was not a revolutionary, that he was an advocate of monarchy, nevertheless, the Anarchists go on trying to "prove" and deem it necessary to go on endlessly trying to "prove" that Hegel was a supporter of "restoration." Why do they do this? Probably, in order by all this to discredit Hegel, to make their readers feel that the method of the "reactionary" Hegel is also "repugnant" and unscientific. If that is so, if Messieurs the Anarchists think they can refute the dialectical method *in this way*, then I must say that *in this way* they can prove nothing but their own simplicity. Pascal and

Leibnitz were not revolutionaries, but the mathematical method they discovered is recognised today as a scientific method; Mayer and Helmholtz were not revolutionaries, but their discoveries in the field of physics became the basis of science; nor were Lamarck and Darwin revolutionaries, but their evolutionary method put biological science on its feet.... Yes, *in this way* Messieurs the Anarchists will prove nothing but their own simplicity.

To proceed. In the opinion of the Anarchists "dialectics is metaphysics" (see *Nobati*, No. 9. Sh. G.), and as they "want to free science from metaphysics, philosophy from theology" (see *Nobati*, No. 3. Sh. G.), they repudiate the dialectical method.

Oh, those Anarchists! As the saying goes: "Blame others for your own sins." Dialectics matured in the struggle against metaphysics and gained fame in this struggle; but according to the Anarchists, "dialectics is metaphysics"! Proudhon, the "father" of the Anarchists, believed that there existed in the world an "immutable justice" established *once and for all* (see Eltzbacher's *Anarchism*, pp. 64-68, foreign edition) and for this Proudhon has been called a metaphysician. Marx fought Proudhon with the aid of the dialectical method and proved that since everything in the world changes, "justice" must also change, and that, consequently, "immutable justice" is metaphysical fantasy (see Marx, *The Poverty of Philosophy*). Yet the Georgian disciples of the metaphysician Proudhon come out and try to "prove" that "dialectics is metaphysics," that metaphysics recognises the "unknowable" and the "thing-in-itself," and in the long run passes into empty theology. In contrast to Proudhon and Spencer, Engels combated metaphysics as well as theology with the aid of the dialectical method (see Engels, *Ludwig Feuerbach* and *Anti-Dühring*). He proved how ridiculously vapid they were. Our Anarchists, however, try to "prove" that Proudhon and Spencer were scientists, whereas Marx and Engels were metaphysicians. One of two things: either Messieurs the Anarchists are deceiving themselves, or they fail to understand what is metaphysics. At all events, the dialectical method is entirely free from blame.

What other accusations do Messieurs the Anarchists hurl against the dialectical method? They say that the dialectical method is "subtle word-weaving," "the method of sophistry," "logical and mental somersaults" (see *Nobati*, No. 8. Sh. G.) "with the aid of which both truth and falsehood are proved with equal facility" (see *Nobati*, No. 4. V. Cherkezishvili).

At first sight it would seem that the accusation advanced by the Anarchists is correct. Listen to what Engels says about the follower of the metaphysical method: "...His communication is: 'Yea yea; nay, nay, for whatsoever is more than these cometh of evil.' For him a thing either exists, or it does not exist; it is equally impossible for a thing to be itself and at the same time something else. Positive and negative absolutely exclude one another..." (see *Anti-Dühring*, Introduction). How is that? – the Anarchist cries heatedly. Is it possible for a thing to be good and bad at the same time?! That is "sophistry," "juggling with words," it shows that "you want to prove truth and falsehood with equal facility!..."

Let us, however, go into the substance of the matter. Today we are demanding a democratic republic. The democratic republic, however, strengthens bourgeois property. Can we say that a democratic republic is good always and everywhere? No, we cannot! Why? Because a democratic republic is good only "*today*," when we are destroying feudal property, but "*tomorrow*," when we shall proceed to destroy bourgeois property and establish socialist property, the democratic republic will no longer be good; on the contrary, it will become a fetter, which we shall smash and cast aside. But as life is in continual motion, as it is impossible to separate the past from the present, and as we are *simultaneously* fighting the feudal rulers and the bourgeoisie, we say: in so far as the democratic republic destroys feudal property it is good and we advocate it, but in so far as it strengthens bourgeois property it is bad, and therefore we criticise it. It follows, therefore, that the democratic republic is simultaneously both "good" and "bad," and thus the answer to the question raised may be both "yes" and "no." It was *facts* of this kind that Engels had in mind when he proved the correctness of the dialectical method in the words quoted above. The Anarchists, however, failed to understand this and to them it seemed to be "sophistry"! The Anarchists are, of course, at liberty to note or ignore these *facts*, they may even ignore the sand on the sandy seashore – they have every right to do that. But why drag in the dialectical method, which, unlike the Anarchists, does not look at life with its eyes shut, which has its finger on the pulse of life and openly says: since life changes, since life is in motion, every phenomenon of life has two trends: a positive and a negative; the first we must defend and the second we must reject? What astonishing people those Anarchists are: they are constantly talking about "justice," but they treat the dialectical method with gross injustice!

To proceed further. In the opinion of our Anarchists, "dialectical development is catastrophic development, by means of which, first the past is utterly destroyed, and then the future is established quite separately.... Cuvier's cataclysms were due to unknown causes, but Marx and Engels's catastrophes are engendered by dialectics" (see *Nobati*, No. 8. Sh. G.). In another place the same author says that "Marxism rests on Darwinism and treats it uncritically" (see *Nobati*, No. 6).

Ponder well over that, reader!

Cuvier rejects Darwin's theory of evolution, he recognises only cataclysms, and cataclysms are *unexpected* upheavals "due to *unknown* causes." The Anarchists say that the Marxists *adhere to Cuvier's view* and therefore *repudiate Darwinism*.

Darwin rejects Cuvier's cataclysms, he recognises gradual evolution. But the same Anarchists say that "Marxism rests on Darwinism and treats it uncritically," therefore, the Marxists *do not advocate Cuvier's cataclysms*.

This is anarchy if you like! As the saying goes: the Sergeant's widow flogged herself! Clearly, Sh. G. of No. 8 of *Nobati* forgot what Sh. G. of No. 6 said. Which is right: No. 6 or No. 8? Or are they both lying?

Let us turn to the facts. Marx says: "At a certain stage of their development, the material productive forces of society come in conflict with the existing relations of production, or – what is but a legal expression for the same thing – with the property relations.... Then begins an epoch of social revolution." But "no social order ever perishes before all the productive forces for which there is room in it have developed..." (see K. Marx, *A Contribution to the Critique of Political Economy*. Preface). If this idea of Marx is applied to modern social life, we shall find that between the present-day productive forces which are *social* in character, and the method of appropriating the product, which is *private* in character, there is a fundamental conflict which must culminate in the socialist revolution (see F. Engels, *Anti-Dühring*, Chapter II, Part III). As you see, in the opinion of Marx and Engels, "revolution" ("catastrophe") is engendered not by Cuvier's "unknown causes," but by very definite and vital social causes called "the development of the productive forces." As you see, in the opinion of Marx and Engels, revolution comes only when the productive forces have sufficiently matured, and not *unexpectedly*, as Cuvier imagined. Clearly, there is nothing in common between Cuvier's cataclysms and the dialectical method. On the other hand, Darwinism repudiates not only Cuvier's cataclysms, but also dialectically conceived revolution, whereas according to the dialectical method evolution and revolution, quantitative and qualitative changes, are two essential forms of the same motion. Clearly, it is also wrong to say that "Marxism... treats Darwinism uncritically." It follows therefore that *Nobati* is lying in both cases, in No. 6 as well as in No. 8.

And so these lying "critics" buttonhole us and go on repeating: Whether you like it or not our lies are better than your truth! Probably they believe that everything is pardonable in an Anarchist.

There is another thing for which Messieurs the Anarchists cannot forgive the dialectical method: "Dialectics... provides no possibility of getting, or jumping, out of oneself, or of jumping over oneself" (see *Nobati*, No. 8. Sh. G.). Now that is the downright truth, Messieurs Anarchists! Here you are absolutely right, my dear sirs: the dialectical method does not provide such a possibility. But why not? Because "jumping out of oneself, or jumping over oneself," is an exercise for wild goats, while the dialectical method was created for human beings. That is the secret!...

Such, in general, are our Anarchists' views on the dialectical method.

Clearly, the Anarchists fail to understand the dialectical method of Marx and Engels; they have conjured up their own dialectics, and it is against this dialectics that they are fighting so ruthlessly.

All we can do is to laugh as we gaze at this spectacle, for one cannot help laughing when one sees a man fighting his own imagination, smashing his own inventions, while at the same time heatedly asserting that he is smashing his opponent.

II

> *"It is not the consciousness of men that determines their being, but, on the contrary, their social being that determines their consciousness."*

Karl Marx

What is the materialist theory?

Everything in the world changes, everything in the world is in motion, but *how* do these changes take place and *in what form* does this motion proceed? – that is the question. We know, for example, that the earth was once an incandescent, fiery mass, then it gradually cooled, then the animal kingdom appeared and developed, then appeared a species of ape from which man subsequently originated. But how did this development take place? Some say that nature and its development were preceded by the universal idea, which subsequently served as the basis of this development, so that the development of the phenomena of nature, it would appear, is merely the *form* of the development of the idea. These people were called idealists, who later split up and followed different trends. Others say that from the very beginning there have existed in the world two opposite forces – idea and matter, and that correspondingly, phenomena are also divided into two categories, the ideal and the material, which are in constant conflict. Thus the development of the phenomena of nature, it would appear, represents a constant struggle between ideal and material phenomena. Those people are called dualists, and they, like the idealists, are split up into different schools.

Marx's materialist theory utterly repudiates both dualism and idealism. Of course, both ideal and material phenomena exist in the world, but this does not mean that they negate each other. On the contrary, the ideal and the material are two different forms of the same phenomenon; they exist together and develop together; there is a close connection between them. That being so, we have no grounds for thinking that they negate each other. Thus, so-called dualism crumbles to its foundations. A single and indivisible nature expressed in two different forms – material and ideal – that is how we should regard the development of nature. A single and indivisible life expressed in two different forms – ideal and material – that is how we should regard the development of life.

Such is the monism of Marx's materialist theory.

At the same time, Marx also repudiates idealism. It is wrong to think that the development of the idea, and of the spiritual side in general, *precedes* nature and the material side in general. So-called external, inorganic nature existed before there were any living beings. The first living matter – protoplasm – possessed no consciousness (idea), it possessed only irritability and the first rudiments of sensation. Later, animals gradually developed the power of sensation, which slowly passed into consciousness, in conformity with the development of their nervous systems. If the ape had never stood upright, if it had always walked on all fours, its descendant – man – would not have been able freely to use his lungs and vocal chords and, therefore, would not have been able to speak; and that would have greatly retarded the development of his consciousness. If, furthermore, the ape had not risen up on its hind legs, its descendant – man – would have been compelled always to look downwards and obtain his impressions only from there; he would have been unable to look up and around himself and, consequently, his brain would have obtained no more material (impressions) than that of the ape; and that would have greatly retarded the development of his consciousness. It follows that the development of the spiritual side is conditioned by the structure of the organism and the development of its nervous system. It follows that the development of the spiritual side, the development of ideas, *is preceded* by the development of the material side, the development of being. Clearly, first the external conditions change, first matter changes, and *then* consciousness and other spiritual phenomena change accordingly – the development of the ideal side *lags behind* the development of material conditions. If we call the material side, the external conditions, being, etc., the *content*, then we must call the ideal side, consciousness and other phenomena of the same kind, the *form*. Hence arose the well-known materialist proposition: in the process of development content precedes form, form lags behind content.

The same must be said about social life. Here, too, material development precedes ideal development, here, too, form lags behind its content. Capitalism existed and a fierce class struggle raged long before scientific socialism was even thought of; the process of production already bore a social character long before the socialist idea arose.

That is why Marx says: "It is not the consciousness of men that determines their being, but, on the contrary, their social being that determines their consciousness" (see K. Marx, *A Contribution to the Critique of Political Economy*). In Marx's opinion, economic development is the material foundation of social life, *its content*, while legal-political and religious-philosophical development is the "*ideological form*" of this content, its "superstructure." Marx, therefore, says: "With the change of the economic foundation the entire immense superstructure is *more or less rapidly* transformed" (*ibid.*).

In social life too, first the external, material conditions change and then the thoughts of men, their world outlook, change. The development of content precedes the rise and development of form. This, of course, does not mean that in Marx's opinion content is possible without form, as Sh. G. imagines (see *Nobati*, No. 1. "A Critique of Monism"). Content is impossible without form, but the point is that since a given form lags behind its content, it never *fully* corresponds to this content; and so the new content is often "obliged" to clothe itself for a time in the old form, and this causes a conflict between them. At the present time, for example, the private character of the appropriation of the product does not correspond to the *social* content of production, and this is the basis of the present-day social "conflict." On the other hand, the conception that the idea is a form of being does not mean that, by its nature, consciousness is the same as matter. That was the opinion held only by the vulgar materialists (for example, Büchner and Moleschott), whose theories fundamentally contradict Marx's materialism, and whom Engels rightly ridiculed in his *Ludwig Feuerbach*. According to Marx's materialism, consciousness and being, mind and matter, are two different forms of the same phenomenon, which, broadly speaking, is called nature. Consequently, they do not negate each other,* but nor are they one and the same phenomenon. The only point is that, in the development of nature and society, consciousness, i.e., what takes place in our heads, is preceded by a corresponding material change, i.e., what takes place outside of us. Any given material change is, sooner or later, inevitably followed by a corresponding ideal change. That is why we

---

* This does not contradict the idea that there is a conflict between form and content. The point is that the conflict is not between content and form in general, but between the *old* form and the *new* content, which is seeking a new form and is striving towards it.

say that an ideal change is the form of a corresponding material change.

Such, in general, is the monism of the dialectical materialism of Marx and Engels.

We shall be told by some: All this may well be true as applied to the history of nature and society. But how do different conceptions and ideas about given objects arise in our heads at the present time? Do so-called external conditions really exist, or is it only our conceptions of these external conditions that exist? And if external conditions exist, to what degree are they perceptible and cognizable?

On this point we say that our conceptions, our "self," exist only in so far as external conditions exist that give rise to impressions in our "self." Whoever unthinkingly says that nothing exists but our conceptions, is compelled to deny the existence of all external conditions and, consequently, must deny the existence of all other people except his own "self," which fundamentally contradicts the main principles of science and vital activity. Yes, external conditions do actually exist; these conditions existed before us, and will exist after us; and the more often and the more strongly they affect our consciousness, the more easily perceptible and cognizable do they become. As regards the question as to how different conceptions and ideas about given objects arise in our heads *at the present time*, we must observe that here we have a repetition in brief of what takes place in the history of nature and society. In this case, too, the object outside of us precedes our conception of it; in this case, too, our conception, the form, lags behind the object, its content, and so forth. When I look at a tree and see it – that only shows that this tree existed even before the conception of a tree arose in my head; that it was this tree that aroused the corresponding conception in my head.

The importance of the monistic materialism of Marx and Engels for the practical activities of mankind can be readily understood. If our world outlook, if our habits and customs are determined by external conditions, if the unsuitability of legal and political forms rests on an economic content, it is clear that we must help to bring about a radical change in economic relations in order, with this change, to bring about a radical change in the habits and customs of the people, and in the political system of the country. Here is what Karl Marx says on that score:

"No great acumen is required to perceive the necessary interconnection of materialism with... socialism. If man constructs all his knowledge, perceptions, etc., from the world of sense... then it follows that it is a question of so arranging the empirical world that he experiences the truly human in it, that he becomes accustomed to experiencing himself as a human being.... If man is unfree in the materialist sense – that is, is free not by reason of the negative force of being able to avoid this or that, but by reason of the positive power to assert his true individuality, then one should not punish individuals for crimes, but rather destroy the anti-social breeding places of crime.... If man is moulded by circumstances, then the circumstances must be moulded humanly" (see *Ludwig Feuerbach*, Appendix: "Karl Marx on the History of French Materialism of the XVIII Century").

Such is the connection between materialism and the practical activities of men.

* * *

What is the anarchist view of the monistic materialism of Marx and Engels?

While Marx's dialectics originated with Hegel, his materialism is a development of Feuerbach's materialism. The Anarchists know this very well, and they try to take advantage of the defects of Hegel and Feuerbach to discredit the dialectical materialism of Marx and Engels. We have already shown with reference to Hegel that these tricks of the Anarchists prove nothing but their own polemical impotence. The same must be said with reference to Feuerbach. For example, they strongly emphasise that "Feuerbach was a pantheist..." that he "deified man..." (see *Nobati*, No. 7. D. Delendi), that "in Feuerbach's opinion man is what he eats..." alleging that from this Marx drew the following conclusion: "Consequently, the main and primary thing is economic conditions," etc. (see *Nobati*, No. 6. Sh. G.). True, nobody has any doubts about Feuerbach's pantheism, his deification of man, and other errors of his of the same kind. On the contrary, Marx and Engels were the first to reveal Feuerbach's errors; nevertheless, the Anarchists deem it necessary once again to "expose" the already exposed errors of Feuerbach. Why? Probably because, in reviling Feuerbach, they want at least in some way to discredit the materialism which Marx borrowed from Feuerbach and then scientifically developed. Could not Feuerbach have had correct as well as erroneous ideas? We say that by tricks of this kind the Anarchists will not shake monistic materialism in the least; all they will do is to prove their own impotence.

The Anarchists disagree among themselves about Marx's materialism. If, for example, we listen to what Mr. Cherkezishvili has to say, it would appear that Marx and Engels detested monistic materialism; in his opinion their materialism is vulgar and not monistic materialism: "The great science of the naturalists, with its system of evolution, transformism and monistic materialism which *Engels so heartily detested...* avoided dialectics," etc. (see *Nobati*, No. 4. V. Cherkezishvili). It follows, therefore, that the natural-scientific materialism, which Cherkezishvili likes and which Engels detested, was monistic materialism. Another Anarchist, however, tells us that the materialism of Marx and Engels is monistic and should therefore be rejected. "Marx's conception of history is a throwback to Hegel. The monistic materialism of absolute subjectivism in general, and Marx's economic monism in particular, are impossible in nature and fallacious in theory.... Monistic materialism is poorly disguised dualism and a compromise between metaphysics and science..." (see *Nobati*, No. 6. Sh. G.).

It would follow that monistic materialism is unacceptable because Marx and Engels, far from detesting it, were actually monistic materialists themselves, and therefore monistic materialism must be rejected.

This is anarchy if you like! They have not yet grasped the substance of Marx's materialism, they have not yet understood whether it is monistic materialism or not, they have not yet agreed among themselves about its merits and demerits, but they already deafen us with their boastful claims: We criticise and raze Marx's materialism to the ground! This by itself shows what grounds their "criticism" can have.

To proceed further. It appears that certain Anarchists are even ignorant of the fact that in science there are various forms of materialism, which differ a great deal from one another: there is, for example, vulgar materialism (in natural science and history), which denies the importance of the ideal side and the effect it has upon the material side; but there is also so-called monistic materialism, which scientifically examines the interrelation between the ideal and the material sides. Some Anarchists confuse all this and at the same time affirm with great aplomb: Whether you like it or not, we subject the materialism of Marx and Engels to devastating criticism! Listen to this: "In the opinion of Engels, and also of Kautsky, Marx rendered mankind a great service in that he..." among other things, discovered the "materialist conception." "Is this true? We do not think so, for we know... that all the historians, scientists and philosophers who adhere to the view that the social mechanism is set in motion by geographic, climatic and telluric, cosmic, anthropological and biological conditions – *are all materialists*" (see *Nobati*, No. 2. Sh. G.). How can you talk to such people? It appears, then, that there is no difference between the "materialism" of Aristotle and of Montesquieu, or between the "materialism" of Marx and of Saint-Simon. A fine example, indeed, of understanding your opponent and subjecting him to devastating criticism!

Some Anarchists heard somewhere that Marx's materialism was a "belly theory" and set about popularising this "idea," probably because paper is cheap in the editorial office of *Nobati* and this process does not cost much. Listen to this: "In the opinion of Feuerbach man is what he eats. This formula had a magic effect on Marx and Engels," and so, in the opinion of the Anarchists, Marx drew from this the conclusion that "consequently the main and primary thing is economic conditions, relations of production...." And then the Anarchists proceed to instruct us in a philosophical tone: "It would be a mistake to say that the sole means of achieving this object (of social life) is eating and economic production.... If *ideology were determined* mainly monistically, by *eating* and economic existence – then some gluttons would be geniuses" (see *Nobati*, No. 6. Sh. G.). You see how easy it is to criticise Marx's materialism! It is sufficient to hear some gossip in the street from some schoolgirl about Marx and Engels, it is sufficient to repeat that street gossip with philosophical aplomb in the columns of a paper like *Nobati*, to leap into fame as a "critic." But tell me one thing, gentlemen: Where, when, in what country, and which Marx did you hear say that "eating determines ideology"? Why did you not cite a single sentence, a single word from the works of Marx to back your accusation? Is economic existence and eating the same thing? One can forgive a schoolgirl, say, for confusing these entirely different concepts, but how is it that you, the "vanquishers of Social-Democracy," "regenerators of science," so carelessly repeat the mistake of a schoolgirl? How, indeed, can eating determine social ideology? Ponder over what you yourselves have said; eating, the form of eating, does not change; in ancient times people ate, masticated and digested their food in the same way as they do now, but the forms of ideology constantly change and develop. Ancient, feudal, bourgeois and proletarian – such are the forms of ideology. Is it conceivable that that which, generally speaking, does not change can determine that which is constantly changing? Marx does, indeed, say that economic existence determines ideology, and this is easy to understand, but is eating and economic existence the same thing? Why do you think it proper to attribute your own foolishness to Marx?

To proceed further. In the opinion of our Anarchists, Marx's materialism "is parallelism...." Or again: "monistic materialism is poorly disguised dualism and a compromise between metaphysics and science...." "Marx drops into dualism because he depicts relations of production as material, and human striving and will as an illusion and a utopia, which, even though it exists, is of no importance" (see *Nobati*, No. 6. Sh. G.). Firstly, Marx's monistic materialism has nothing in common with silly parallelism. From the standpoint of materialism, the material side, content, necessarily *precedes* the ideal side, form. Parallelism repudiates this view and emphatically affirms that neither the material nor the ideal *comes first*, that both move together, parallel with each other. Secondly, what is there in common between Marx's monism and dualism when we know perfectly well (and you, Messieurs Anarchists, should also know this if you read Marxist literature!) that the former springs from *one principle* – nature, which has a material and an ideal form, whereas the latter springs from *two principles* – the material and the ideal which, according to dualism, mutually negate each other. Thirdly, who said that "human striving and will are not important"? Why don't you point to the place where Marx says that? Does not Marx speak of the importance of "striving and will" in his *Eighteenth Brumaire of Louis Bonaparte*, in his *Class Struggles in France*, in his *Civil War in France*, and in other pamphlets? Why, then, did Marx try to develop the proletarians' "will and striving" in the socialist spirit, why did he conduct propaganda among them if he attached no importance to "striving and will"? Or, what did Engels talk about in his well-known articles of 1891-94 if not the "importance of striving and will"? Human striving and will acquire their content from economic existence, but that does not mean that they exert no influence on the development of economic relations. Is it really so difficult for our Anarchists to digest this simple idea? It is rightly said that a passion for criticism is one thing, but criticism itself is another.

Here is another accusation Messieurs the Anarchists make: "form is inconceivable without content..." therefore, one cannot say that "form lags behind content... they 'co-exist.'... Otherwise, monism would be an absurdity" (see *Nobati*, No. 1. Sh. G.). Messieurs the Anarchists are somewhat confused. Content is inconceivable without form, but the *existing form* never fully corresponds to the existing content; to a certain extent the new content is always clothed in the old form, as a consequence, there is always a conflict between the old form and the new content. It is precisely on this ground that revolutions occur, and this, among other things, expresses the revolutionary spirit of Marx's materialism. The Anarchists, however, have failed to understand this and obstinately repeat that there is no content without form....

Such are the Anarchists' views on materialism. We shall say no more. It is sufficiently clear as it is that the Anarchists have invented their own Marx, have ascribed to him a "materialism" of their own invention, and are now fighting this "materialism." But not a single bullet of theirs hits the true Marx and the true materialism....

What connection is there between dialectical materialism and proletarian socialism?

Akhali Tskhovreba
(*New Life*), Nos. 2, 4,
7 and 16, June 21, 24
and 28 and July 9, 1906

Signed: *Koba*

Translated from the Georgian

NOTES

[1] At the end of 1905 and the beginning of 1906, a group of Anarchists in Georgia, headed by the well-known Anarchist and follower of Kropotkin, V. Cherkezishvili and his supporters Mikhako Tsereleli (Bâton), Shalva Gogelia (Sh. G.) and others conducted a fierce campaign against the Social-Democrats. This group published in Tiflis the newspapers *Nobati, Musha* and others. The Anarchists had no support among the proletariat, but they achieved some success among the declassed and petty-bourgeois elements. J. V. Stalin wrote a series of articles against the Anarchists under the general title of *Anarchism or Socialism?* The first four instalments appeared in *Akhali Tskhovreba* in June and July 1906. The rest were not published as the newspaper was suppressed by the authorities. In December 1906 and on January 1, 1907, the articles that were published in *Akhali Tskhovreba* were reprinted in *Akhali Droyeba*, in a slightly revised form, with the following editorial comment: "Recently, the Office Employees' Union wrote to us suggesting that we should publish articles on anarchism, socialism, and cognate questions (see *Akhali Droyeba*, No. 3). The same wish was expressed by several other comrades. We gladly meet these wishes and publish these articles. Regarding them, we think it necessary to mention that some have already appeared in the Georgian press (but for reasons over which the author had no control, they were not completed). Nevertheless we considered it necessary to reprint all the articles in full and requested the author to rewrite them in a more popular style, and this he gladly did." This explains the two versions of the first four instalments of *Anarchism or Socialism?* They were continued in the newspapers *Chveni Tskhovreba* in February 1907, and in *Dro* in April 1907. The first version of the articles *Anarchism or Socialism?* as published in *Akhali Tskhovreba* is given as an appendix to the present volume.

Chveni Tskhovreba (*Our Life*) – a daily Bolshevik newspaper published legally in Tiflis under the direction of J. V. Stalin, began publication on February 18, 1907. In all, thirteen numbers were issued. It was suppressed on March 6, 1907, for its "extremist trend."

Dro (*Time*) – a daily Bolshevik newspaper published in Tiflis after the suppression of *Chveni Tskhovreba*, ran from March 11 to April 15, 1907, under the direction of J. V. Stalin. M. Tskhakaya and M. Davitashvili were members of the editorial board. In all, thirty-one numbers were issued.

[2] *Nobati* (*The Call*) – a weekly newspaper published by the Georgian Anarchists in Tiflis in 1906.

[3] Karl Marx and Frederick Engels, *Selected Works*, Vol. II, Moscow 1951, p. 328.

[4] Karl Marx and Frederick Engels, *Selected Works*, Vol. I, Moscow 1951, p. 329.

[5] See Karl Marx and Friedrich Engels, *Die heilige Familie*, "Kritische Schlacht gegen den französischen Materialismus." (Marx-Engels, *Gesamtausgabe*, Erste Abteilung, Band 3, S. 307-08.)

[6] See Karl Marx, *Misère de la Philosophie*. (Marx-Engels, *Gesamtausgabe*, Erste Abteilung, Band 6, S. 227.)

[7] See Karl Marx and Frederick Engels, *Selected Works*, Vol. II, Moscow 1951, p. 292.

[8] See Karl Marx and Frederick Engels, *Selected Works*, Vol. II, Moscow 1951, p. 23.

[9] See Frederick Engels, *Herr Eugen Dühring's Revolution in Science* (*Anti-Dühring*), Moscow 1947, pp. 233-35.

[10] *Musha* (*The Worker*) – a daily newspaper published by the Georgian Anarchists in Tiflis in 1906.

[11] *Khma* (*The Voice*) – a daily newspaper published by the Georgian Anarchists in Tiflis in 1906.

[12] Karl Marx, *The Cologne Trial of the Communists*, published by *Molot* Publishers, St. Petersburg, 1906, p. 113 (IX. Appendix. *Address of the Central Committee to the Communist League*, March, 1850). (See Karl Marx and Frederick Engels, *Selected Works*, Vol. I, Moscow 1951, pp. 104-05.)

[13] See Karl Marx and Frederick Engels, *Selected Works*, Vol. II, Moscow 1951, p. 420.

[14] The author quotes this passage from Karl Marx's pamphlet *The Civil War in France*, with a preface by F. Engels, Russian translation from the German edited by N. Lenin, 1905 (see Karl Marx and Frederick Engels, *Selected Works*, Vol. I, Moscow 1951, p. 440).

63592759R00053

Made in the USA
Middletown, DE
26 August 2019